Donated By

Cameron C. Nickels

Civil War Humor

◊ ◊ ◊

CIVIL WAR
HUMOR

Cameron C. Nickels

University Press of Mississippi / Jackson

www.upress.state.ms.us

Page iii: "The Way Lincoln Will Be Lifted
out of Washington City by General Lee."
From *Southern Punch* (30 April 1864).

The University Press of Mississippi is a member
of the Association of American University Presses.

First printing 2010
∞
Library of Congress Cataloging-in-Publication Data

Nickels, Cameron C.
Civil War humor / Cameron C. Nickels.
p. cm.
Includes bibliographical references and index.
ISBN 978-1-60473-747-9 (cloth : alk. paper) —
ISBN 978-1-60473-748-6 (ebook) 1. American wit
and humor—History and criticism. 2. United States—
History—Civil War, 1861–1865—Humor. 3. United
States—History—Civil War, 1861–1865—Literature
and the war. I. Title.
PS437.N53 2010
817'.409358731—dc22   2010005358

British Library Cataloging-in-Publication Data available

For Thomas D. Catte,
who was always there, to the end

Contents

Chapter Three

CIVIL WAR, WAR HUMOR

Chapter Four

THE AFRICAN AMERICAN IN CIVIL WAR HUMOR

Preface

It is probably safe to say that more books have been published about the Civil War than any other subject in American history. So I was surprised a few years ago while looking over the bounty of books on all kinds of arcane topics at a bookstore in Gettysburg, Pennsylvania, that I saw nothing on humor of the Civil War. Although no expert on that conflict, as a literary historian who had spent most of his professional career writing about American humor, I did know that quite a bit of humor had been published. I knew, too, that much had been written about the major humorists of that period—Charles Farrar Browne ("Artemus Ward"), David Ross Locke ("Petroleum V. Nasby"), Robert Henry Newell ("Orpheus C. Kerr"), and Charles H. Smith ("Bill Arp")—but what about the thousands of stories, songs, cartoons, and visual humor of many kinds? I owned Sylvia G. L. Dannett's *A Treasury of Civil War Humor* (1963), primarily a good anthology with introductory comments to different genres, including pictorial envelopes and comic valentines, all of it in a format that features the graphics to good advantage, albeit black and white. I ordered Paul Zall's *Blue and Gray Laughing* (1996), a chronological arrangement of brief stories and illustrations, most of them from periodicals. Zall does cite his sources, but at times inaccurately, and silently edits some. Facing retirement, I decided that I would add yet another Civil War book to the shelf.

Years earlier, when I was writing a book on nineteenth-century New England humor, I got used to people asking, with some irony, maybe sarcasm, "Oh, there *was* some?" Somehow, though, I did not anticipate the same response when I said I was writing a book on Civil War humor. This time the question seemed not so much ironic, but doubtful about how war could be humorous. Well, there was a great deal of Civil War humor in many forms, but the point is not that this war, or any war, is laughable, but that humor provides a way of dealing with something so literally and figuratively devastating, even horrific, in so many ways. And that is what this book is about.

Anyone who writes a serious book about any kind of humor has to consider the most basic question on the subject: "What *is* 'humor'?" which is another way of asking "What is *humorous*?" Any answer is complicated, because the responses to humor are at the same time intellectual, emotional, and even physiological, and so theories abound in several academic disciplines. Humor is something that makes us react not necessarily with laughter, maybe only a smile, but we do react because we see something that strikes us as amusing, funny, however we might express it. ("Risible" is a fine word, but not in common enough usage.) In any case, somehow we sense that we "get it," that we recognize what the author, speaker, or artist wants us to see as humorous.

Two other, rather different, responses interest me here, though, because in this book I want to go from "getting" Civil War humor to "understanding" something about it and its role in the culture at the time, and that is more complex. For one thing, we may well get what the author intended as humorous but not think it so at all; we might frown rather than smile. Much in Civil War humor is racist, for example, even when that is not intended, but there is much to be learned about the past, and maybe the present, too, for all that. Another very different response is that we do not get at all what is intended as humorous, even though where it was published, a caption, or something about the format signals that it is. Then we neither smile nor frown, but scratch our head.

In either case, in order first to get the humor and then to understand something about it, that humor needs to be explained, analyzed. Ah, "But when you *analyze* humor," we humor scholars are told archly, "it is no longer humorous!" (Implied is that we have no sense of humor. Which may be true; see the story below.) And yet, to analyze is exactly what anyone does, very quickly and therefore unconsciously, for anything to be humorous, such as a cartoon, a scene in a movie or sitcom, a joke. We get it and think it is funny; we get it and do not think it is; or we just do not get it, period. Think of a political cartoon and all that has to be put together in order to get the humor: the historical background, the conventions of the form, and the broad strokes of caricature, for examples. People during the Civil War did the same thing with what their popular culture offered them as humorous. They may not have thought it funny in the sense of agreeing with it, but they probably got that it was meant to be. Today we have some difficulty with that humor, and so explanations are necessary, not only to get it but also to understand something about it. For example, I think this is funny:

> Some Indiana soldiers on a scout in the mountains of Georgia, came upon a house occupied by an old woman. "Well, old lady," said the leader, "what are you? secesh?" "No," "Union, then?" "No," said she. "What then?" "Baptist," said she, promptly, "and always was." (*Keene [New Hampshire] Sentinel,* 24 March 1864)

Having tried this out on people, I found that while they might know if she is being asked if she sides with the Union, the story has no chance of being humorous unless they know that she is also asked if she is a Confederate, "secesh." Knowing *that,* someone might find her answer, "Baptist," mildly amusing, but I think there is something to learn about the place of this story, where it might *fit* in the context of the Civil War. People at the time apparently thought the story was funny, appearing as it did in slightly different forms in newspapers of the North and South (and San Francisco in the West) from 1861 to 1864. We do not know *why* it was funny to so many, but—and here comes the analysis—I think it has something to do with the characterization of a wise old woman who knows better than to admit to any national loyalties, so she answers, "promptly," with a non sequitur, "Baptist." The real crux of the humor, though, is that the humorist behind it all (this is not a news story) punctuates her good sense with that delayed "and always was." The readers of the time, I believe, laughed ruefully, if only for a moment, at the meaninglessness of national loyalties in a "civil" war, a conclusion consistent with other sources of the time. This is not to say that there are not other conclusions that could be made about the story, but any analysis potentially enriches our understanding of the humor in its context. And does not destroy it.

"Understanding," then, means that I am not so much interested in the "facts" of the war—its causes, battles, politics, and personalities, and so forth—as I am in getting some sense of how all of that and more gets interpreted by popular culture to create what Alice Fahs calls the "imagined" Civil War. In *The Imagined Civil War: Popular Literature of the North & South, 1861–1865* (2001), Fahs shows lucidly and in so many new ways how popular culture of so many kinds created an iconography and a rhetoric that both reflected and shaped the cultural and political meanings of the war for the people then—a dynamic process because the war evolved over time and the meanings changed. Fahs's chapter on humor deals well and originally with the work of the four major war humorists, which she sees in terms of the imaginative power of "serious" popular culture—the sentimental and patriotic—and the many forms it took in what I call in my introduction a "paper war."

In this book, I want to look into humor published during the war and come to some sense of its role in shaping and reflecting the cultural imagination about it. Humor shared much the same rhetoric and iconography of serious popular literature and can in many respects be read as the flip-side, maybe the alter-ego, of that literature. Humor, for example, poked fun at the excesses of sentimentality in popular culture. Dozens of songs were devoted to "mother" as the ultimate embodiment of heartfelt feelings, but "Mother on the Brain," by using over thirty-six titles of such songs in the verses, draws attention to and pokes fun at their emotional indulgence. ("On the brain" was a popular catch phrase for a foolish obsession.) As the first lines say, "As you look upon the songs that you see now-a-days, / The gentle words of Mother will surely meet your gaze." Even the most popular song of this type both North and South, "Dear Mother, I've Come Home to Die," was comically parodied with the more realistic "Mother, I've Come Home to Eat." Although none of these parodies were as popular as the originals, they reveal a willingness, perhaps a need, to undercut the high seriousness of the originals and to relieve it humorously. As Lincoln told his sober-sided cabinet, urging them to read the humor of Artemus Ward, "With the fearful strain that is upon me night and day, if I did not laugh I should die, and you need this medicine as much as I do" (quoted in Seitz 1919, 114).

Because I wanted to get some sense of the place of humor in the war, it was imperative that I use texts (written and visual) published from the fall of Fort Sumter in April 1861 to the end of the war in May 1865. Doing so proved more difficult than I originally thought. Personal writings—letters, diaries, and memoirs—can be unreliable unless published during the war years (and little of it was), as Bell I. Wiley discusses cogently in his classic books, *The Life of Johnny Reb* (1943) and *The Life of Billy Yank* (1952). Much the same is true with many potentially promising sources published in the years *after* the war that were marketed as being *of* the war. Many books published since have perpetuated that error. The Civil War in the popular imagination after that conflict is certainly a significant cultural question, but not the one I want to take up here. Fortunately, a growing number of primary texts of many kinds are available on the Internet, which

makes it possible not only to see them as originals but also to verify
their publication during the war years. Even more useful are contemporary newspapers on the Internet that can be searched for humor
not published in national magazines. Newspapers also give insight
into the contemporary context for understanding that humor.

After reading everything I could find, I faced the problem of making
some kind of organizational sense of it all. Chronology had an immediate appeal because it appeared so easy, was truly objective, and also
might reveal, or at least suggest, something meaningful to the war as it
evolved. I do think that is often true toward the end of the war, but too
many texts—song sheets, broadsides, comic valentines, and pictorial
covers—are undated. Also, even dated material was often reprinted
and the first appearance not known. I also thought of a basic Union-
Confederate division, and while there are major differences in what
I call here "humor on the home front," not only is humor on other
topics often non-partisan, but it appeared in the North as well as the
South. I toyed for some time with arranging selections by genre, such
as "Poems," "Stories," "Songs," "Illustrations," and so forth. Nearing
completion of a rough draft for a chapter on songs, though, I realized
that much of what I had said about the humor there would need to be
repeated in other chapters. Putting it all together under topics that
are the chapters here addressed these problems and, I believe, comes
closer to how readers during the war would have "experienced" humor:
on many topics, in several genres, and from a variety of sources.

Acknowledgments

My name is on the title page of this book because I wrote all of the words in it, but anybody who has done it knows that the words could not have been written without the help of many people. This part of the book is where I try to acknowledge that.

There are two stages to writing a book; the second is writing itself, and it is not much fun, and (maybe "because") it has to be solitary. By far the most enjoyable stage is doing the research, gathering up what the words will be about, and for this book that meant finding and reading as many examples of humor published during and about the Civil War as I could. And *that* was enjoyable because research is not solitary but a community effort, which meant meeting and working with people who not only helped me with what I was doing but seemed to enjoy doing it.

It all started the year I retired from James Madison University, where Shawn Miller, a student assistant in the department, copied, typed, and looked things up. He must have enjoyed it because he went to graduate school to get a doctorate in English. In the years that followed, the Department of English let me use its machines and paper, and the Interlibrary Loan Department of Carrier Library found things I needed. As someone whose high school graduation present was a Royal typewriter, I particularly appreciated the Center for Instructional Technology for patiently helping me make digitalized illustrations appear on the screen and, ultimately, in this book.

Serious research (perhaps oxymoronic) began the summer after retirement as a McClean Contributing Fellow at the Library Company of Philadelphia, where I was required to immerse myself for a month into the extraordinary John A. McAllister Collection of Civil War Era Printed Ephemera, Graphics, and Manuscripts. The second day there, I had to ask: "So I get to come back tomorrow and every day after that for a month—and get paid?" "Yes." Like all librarians and archivists I would ultimately work with, they knew their stuff there and enthusiastically helped me do mine better. Surely the ultimate in research as "community" took place when I gave my research-in-progress report at an informal lunch meeting: those who attended were willing to sing, with gusto, even, "Maryland, My Maryland" and its parodies. (See my introduction.)

Working at the American Antiquarian Society was like going home. I had started my research in American (New England) humor there over three decades earlier and made several pilgrimages over the following years. Like the Library Company of Philadelphia, it is one of the very top research libraries in Americana and has personable professionals to guide you through it all. They, and the people at every library or archive where I worked, helped me put it together at the end.

I dearly and sincerely love libraries and the professionals who staff them, but I also have to say something about the wealth of primary resources available on the Internet. This is solitary work, true, but finding the Lester Levy Collection of sheet music at the Johns Hopkins University Web site; broadsides and sheet music at Duke and Wake Forest Universities; the American Memory database at the Library of Congress; and facsimile editions of so many books—all of these and more made me whoop with joy, alone at the keyboard. Virtually all of the primary sources I use here were found with a good "Google," a verb that my spell-checker still flags. There are no people per se to thank for this bounty, but bless them and the institutions that support their work.

The Internet did fail me when it came to comic valentines, but I did find the name of Nancy Rosen, the authority on valentines in general (president of the National Valentine Collectors Association says it all, but not really). And she put me in touch with "Dreadful" Marcia Richards, a collector of "penny dreadfuls" (as comic valentines were called), so devoted that she insists upon the "Dreadful" in her name. She sent me digital copies of her Civil War collection, and although I have used only three of them in this book, they deserve one of their own.

◊ ◊ ◊

Ultimately, despite the good times, I had to try to make some sense out of what I found, and that meant writing. And although solitary work (but not necessarily lonely), I did need to reach out to a different community, one of long-standing for the most part. Professor John J. O'Neill of Hamilton College (friend from graduate school) and Professor Scott Suter of Bridgewater College (former student and still friend) responded when I asked if something I wanted to use was humorous and if what I wanted to say about it made sense. Professor Robin McNallie (friend and former officemate) gave me his usual careful reading of what I wrote when I had been at it so long that it started making little sense to me. Friend Jeb Swarztentruber was my computer guru, guiding me through the many electronic vicissitudes, including answering late-night calls of "Help!" Finally, literally and figuratively, Lt. Col. John R. Buschmann, USAF (Ret.), and Terry Weatherford, former SFC, USA Infantry, read some of what I had written to give me an idea of whether Civil War enthusiasts could make some sense out of what I had written.

As I said at the beginning, the words here are mine, but they would not be here without the community of people, many of whom I have never met, or only briefly, or we only corresponded.

Civil War Humor

Introduction

CIVIL WAR HUMOR, A PAPER WAR

The war from 1861 to 1865 coincided and had much to do with further-ing the modernization of an inexpensive print mass medium, a phe-nomenon of popular culture that would not be equaled for a century, when another war would do the same for the video medium. In each case, the medium responded to the interest in the war at the same time that it mediated that interest and co-modified it. In the North telegraphy meant that the latest news could be made available for eager and anxious consumers, while railroads delivered illustrations from the battle front. Of the war fever that infected non-combatants eager for information, "It is not a breathless courier who comes back with the report of the army we have lost sight of for a month, nor a single bulletin which tells us all we are to know for a week of some great engagement," Oliver Wendell Holmes wrote in September 1861, "but almost hourly paragraphs, laden with truth or falsehood as the case may be, making us restless always for the last fact or rumor they are telling" (1891, 7). And not only news: advances in lithography and printing generally meant that the public appetite could be fed quickly and inexpensively in a wide variety of saleable forms. (Three days after the fall of Fort Sumter, for example, George Root had written and pub-lished the first war-related song.) Broadsides and song sheets, politi-cal cartoons, pictorial envelopes, trading cards, and comic valentines were printed in the thousands and sold, often literally, for pennies. Inexpensive too were book series, such as T. R. Dawley's *Camp and Fireside Library*, *Incidents of American Camp Life*, *Fun for the Camp*, and *Leslie's Pictorial History of the War*, as well as song books, board games, and paper dolls, all of it patriotic, but everything a salable commod-ity. Pointing to advertisements soon after war began for Union but-tons with appropriate portraits, Union pins, badges, rosettes, chromo lithographs, and more, Alice Fahs writes, "It was possible to connect

PERTINENT QUESTIONS!

Why does Jefferson Davis look so thin?

Why is Stephens so singularly boney?

Can you tell me? I mean **YOU** whose eyes now rest on these lines! What! you shake your head as if you did not know. *Well, well, "where did you come from?"* Any one who gave a moments thought to the subject might have *known.* The only reason that can account for this, is *THE FACT* that neither of them have ever called at

M. Samstag's,

Nos. 462 and 464 Seventh street,

(Opposite the Post Office,)

And **CONSEQUENTLY** neither have ever tasted his life-giving, appetite provoking

☞CREAM ALE AND PORTER

which will give any man, with a soul in his body, about 10 pounds of flesh per month. Doubt it, do you? Well, now just try it, and if it does not convince **YOU** in 30 days, why, then you or any other man can't be fattened by mortal means.

"That's what's the matter!"

You want the directions do you? Well, here it is,

M. SAMSTAG, 462 and 464 Seventh street,

Opposite the Post Office, is the place.

H. Polkinhorn's Steam Job Printing Office, D street, bet. 6th & 7th sts., Washington, D. C.

"Pertinent Questions!"
Courtesy of the Library
of Congress.

buying a wide range of goods with being loyal to the nation" (2001, 4). Some advertisements went further in anticipating modern merchandising in making only the most tenuous connection between the product and patriotism. No war rhetoric in "Pertinent Questions!"; the slightly built Confederate president and vice president (Alexander Stephens weighed in at less than a hundred pounds) are, ironically, potential customers for the restorative powers of M. Samstag's "life-giving, appetite provoking" cream ale and porter.

The disadvantages of the Confederacy in this paper war were distinct and profound, as its partisans well knew. Before 1861, the South had relied on the North to supply not only much of the content but, more crucially, virtually all of the printing infrastructure, the physical necessities of printing. When the conflict began, there was only one Southern foundry (in Nashville) capable of forging type, no manufacturers of printing presses, few paper mills, and no means of making paper from wood pulp. In addition, the Union blockade of shipping early in the war created shortages of all kinds, and printing had to be done with ersatz ink; and, indeed, newspapers were printed on wallpaper, wrapping paper, and the backs of business forms. Qualified artisans were in short supply as well. "A well-illustrated magazine *cannot* yet be produced in the South," the *Southern Monthly* (March 1862) admitted. "Good artists we can procure, but good engravers on wood are scarce among us," and it went on to confess that "the wood itself is not be had." (With no engraver capable of rendering the new, official Confederate seal, the work had to be done in Scotland.) Over time, with the great majority of battles taking place on Confederate soil, publishing centers were occupied by Union troops, and lines of communication were disrupted. Finally, the military draft in the Confederacy cut a wider swath than it did in the Union, creating a shortage of printers, illustrators, and editors.

Humor and Songs

In the paper war, music in the Confederacy "far outstripped every other area of Southern publishing during the war, expanding dramatically in response to popular demand," Drew Gilpin Faust writes (1988, 18). Richard B. Harwell explains why: "Cheap to produce and requiring comparatively small investment in scarce supplies of paper, song sheets could be distributed more easily than books." Thus, Confederate music imprints "are more than five times the numbers of novels, plays, and other books of pleasure" (1950, 4).[1]

Already popular throughout America in the 1850s in homes and formal glee clubs, singing became even more so during the war years, what with the need for soldiers and those at home to express vocally the wide array of conflicting feelings that the conflict evoked. (And they would have heard many of them sung on stage.) Charles Leland's "War Songs and Their Influence in History," in the *United States Service Magazine* (January 1864), stated that he had "heard from a collector that during the first year of the present war two thousand songs were published upon it, and the subsequent rate of increase has been somewhat greater!" Surely an inflated figure, but not entirely if one considers the various forms that songs took— song sheet broadsides as well as sheet music. Certainly the war did something to promote singing. George Root, a major Chicago song-smith and publisher of sheet music, wrote in his autobiography, "The growth of our business after the war commenced was something remarkable," and "when the war closed the war songs stopped as if they had been shot" (1891, 139, 151).

The songs of the Civil War appeared in three major forms. The greatest numbers by far were song sheets, or "penny ballads," as they were also called, with new, topical lyrics put to traditional airs. Cheap, quickly printed, at times with typographical errors and unmediated by editorial review, song sheets, like broadsides, provided quick responses to events and people significant at the moment. Also, as with poetic broadsides, the verse was usually doggerel, but even today that gives a vibrant immediacy to the topic.

Much the same kind of material—old favorites and contemporary lyrics put to familiar airs—appeared in pocket-sized song books or "songsters," as they were called. Like song sheets, they had been around before the war, but publishers North and South printed dozens of these inexpensive collections for a new market, with titles such as *The Camp-fire Companion; A Choice Collection of Songs for the Soldier* (1861), *Songs of the Soldiers* (1864), and *The Campfire Songster* (1862). The subtitle of *The Heart and Home Songster* (1862) sums up nicely the many types of songs that these collections offered and the variety of emotional responses to the war: "Containing a choice collection of songs of the affections, and embracing all the most popular and fashionable, comic, convivial, moral, sentimental and patriotic songs."

"Contraband Waltz."
Courtesy of the Lester S.
Levy Collection, The
Sheridan Libraries, The
Johns Hopkins University.

Inexpensive, small, and thus easy to carry, these collections had a meaningful place in the daily lives of soldiers. "We kept song books with us and passed much of our leisure time singing," a Virginia soldier wrote; "I carried my book even through prison and brought it home with me" (Wiley 1943, 379 n. 5). A poignant sense of the role that these songsters played in the war can be experienced by the researcher today who handles them with mandatory white cotton gloves in the special collections of research libraries: despite the many dozens of titles printed in the tens of thousands, these songsters are among the rarest of Civil War memorabilia, and extant copies are fragile, often lacking covers as well as pages.

Sheet music made for a different kind of experience for those on the home front. True parlor music, it was written as a piano solo or to be sung in parts with musical accompaniment. Sheet music was more expensive because it provided the musical score in addition to the lyrics and therefore required more sophisticated technology and a greater investment in typefaces and engraving. More expensive too because, unlike penny ballads that had generic illustrations, if any, sheet music featured original artwork for the cover page that gave additional, iconic meaning, even when the piece was an instrumental. A striking example of this is the one-page "Contraband Waltz" and "'Skedaddle' Grand March," where the notes on the staff are stick figures of African Americans, whose black or white clothing indicates the type of note it is, i.e., a quarter or a half note.

Whatever form songs took, the great majority written and sung during the war were serious—sentimental or patriotic—not comic. True, the lyrics to serious war songs were often so mawkish that they seem laughable to readers today, and to those of the time as well, it would appear, given the number of humorous parodies of those songs.

Music and Humor, an Aside

When we look at Civil War songs today, we tend to give our attention to the words, as distinct from the music, or tunes, the words were sung to. (True, Civil War re-enactors sing and have recorded dozens of these songs.) We pretty much have to because we do not know those "airs," as tunes were called then. But we need to remember that in their own time, songs were oral, aural, and participatory: meant to be sung aloud with other people or heard in a theater. Today, we *read* the lyrics of Civil War songs, both serious and humorous, as poetry, which is to say silently, passively. (We should read poems aloud more than we do, to give meaning, and they surely were back then.) Poetic form itself can make the words more humorous or serious because the rigid structure of rhythm and rhyme sets up expectations into which the words fit: the more imaginative in fulfilling those expectations, the more satisfying the result, evoking the last tear of a serious poem or the last chuckle in a humorous one. Reading the words aloud, in turn, means interpreting those sentiments vocally in one's own way, ultimately, in various ways.

The addition of music, however, calls for not only vocalizing and thus interpreting those sentiments but doing so in terms of the musical notes. To get some sense today of the connection between music and humor of the war, we need a tune still familiar. "Dixie" is certainly that, but there are too many different texts, Union and Confederate. One tune, though, is familiar enough to give us an idea of how music can work with poetic form to enhance the sentiments of the lyrics— again, serious or humorous.

Written in April 1861 to protest the passage of Union troops through Baltimore on their way to the Capitol, the poem "Maryland,

My Maryland" was set to the tune "Tannenbaum, O Tannenbaum," which everybody sings today as "O Christmas Tree, O Christmas Tree." "Maryland, My Maryland" quickly became one of the most popular songs of the Confederacy, an early candidate for a national anthem. The song begins with a dramatic image, made all the more so by the stately tune, and the reader can get some sense of what music adds by singing (perhaps best done alone) the following opening lines:

> The despot's heel is on thy shore,
> Maryland, my Maryland!
> His torch is at thy temple door,
> Maryland, my Maryland!
> Avenge the patriotic gore,
> That flecked the streets of Baltimore,
> And be the battle queen of yore,
> Maryland, my Maryland!

The high seriousness of the words can be amplified by singing them in that way. Say, for example, the note for the first syllable of "patriotic," the highest note in the song and the note held longest in the middle of a line, it yearns for vocal, that is, musical, expression. The refrain does too, parsing out the syllables of the words with the rise and then fall of notes.

The Union "Answer to 'My Maryland'" was one of many parodies of the Confederate favorite. (This should be sung too.)

> The Rebel feet are on our shore,
> Maryland! My Maryland!
> I smell 'em half a mile or more,
> Maryland! My Maryland!
> Their shockless hordes are at my door,
> Their drunken generals on my floor,
> What now can sweeten Baltimore?
> Maryland! My Maryland!

The lyrics are humorous, a parody, because the writer uses many of the same and similar words of the original but reverses their meanings. "Despot's heel" in the first line, for example, gets replaced with "Rebel feet," which becomes the satiric motif for the stanza (for the song as a whole, in fact), a common Union characterization of Confederate soldiers as unwashed rubes. Humorous as well are the reversals of the expectations created by the melody, humor that a singer can play with by various vocal interpretations of the notes, such as sarcastic exaggeration. The dramatic note of the first syllable of the original "patriot" now emphasizes the very different word "horde," and the use of the same words for the refrain repeatedly underscores the parodic reversals of the original verses.

◊ ◊ ◊

With songs, we have the clearest window into the popular imagination and the Civil War. For one thing, most of them are not only extant but readily available on the Internet, and they were highly popular, with song sheets printed in the thousands. Sheet music was more expensive, purchased to be sung in homes with other people and piano accompaniment. In our mind's eye we can see them holding these songs and in our mind's ear get some sense of the social harmony in their vocally articulating the words.

Pictorial Envelopes

Pictorial, or "patriotic," envelopes—envelopes with drawings and brief verbal captions—first appeared in the 1850s as advertisements with company logos and slogans. After 1861, however, they became a highly popular way of visually expressing and sharing patriotic and political convictions, often satirically. Stephen W. Berry says that "their use of vivid imagery to manipulate the emotions and secure the allegiance of a civilian population marked an important first in the development of wartime propaganda" (1998, 64). Pictorial envelopes were also a popular collectable, sometimes sold as a series featuring military scenes, battles, and camp life. Estimates of the number of Union designs range widely, from 5,000 to 15,000, and the Southern contrast to Northern production points up again the disparity of resources, with perhaps 150 basic Confederate designs, and the great majority of those appearing before 1863 (Weiss 1995, 7; Wishnietsky 1991, 142). Many published in the North represented the satiric view of pro-Southern sympathizers, but virtually none in the South were humorous. The most popular designs there were flags, making a visual affirmation of Confederate unity.

Comic Valentines

Sending valentines had been around for centuries, since the time of the saint who, according to tradition, inspired it. And, no doubt, there had long been those who went against the traditional, loving grain. We do know that sending valentines started to become popular around the turn of the nineteenth century in Britain and America. The earliest were handmade, and even when manufactured valentines first came on the market, good taste deemed that the message should be penned by the sender. Publishers, however, had marketed for some time "Valentine Writers" to provide verses "for every taste, from the heavy sentimental, the comic, down to the lewd" (Staff 1966, 47). By mid-century both "sentimentals" and "comics" were in mass production, and messages became as stereotyped as the pictures. Ruth Webb Lee quotes Phillip J. Cozans, a major New York valentine publisher, as saying that over three million valentines were published in 1847, with sales nearly equally divided between the two types (Lee 1952, 89). "Vinegar valentines," or "penny dreadfuls," as the comic ones were also called, were tasteless, even vulgar, and sent anonymously to drunks, shrews, bachelors, old maids, dandies, flirts, penny-pinchers, and the like. (Adding insult to insult, recipients paid the postage.) An article in *The Joker* (17 February 1855), speaking of the pleasantries and tender conventions of giving valentines, ends with an admonition:

> We advise our readers to avoid marring the original observance of the anniversary by sending satirical epistles to those who have been prevented by age or ugliness from shining in the Court of Cupid. Such documents are spiteful, wicked and indefensible. They often inflict much pain, and sometimes create ill feelings which lead to lamentable disagreements, and enmities which are never healed.

As it did for so many aspects of popular culture, the Civil War created a new niche market for publishers of valentines both serious and comic. The separating of lovers and sons along with the very real dangers of war itself created poignantly new circumstances for everyone, while comic valentines found their way to shirkers, martial posturing, and chicanery. T. J. Strong, an engraver and publisher, advertised in the *New York Herald* (January 1863) a variety of options in his "Soldier's Valentine Packets," including "1 very fancy Valentine, new style," "2 fancy Valentine cards," "1 elegant embossed envelope," and "3 military comic Valentines, new style." Given their more pungent message, comic valentines were neither "fancy" nor "embossed" but printed on a full page dominated by a figure drawn in the broad strokes of caricature. Adding to the effect were basic, bold colors done by hand or with multiple printings. Lines of verse at the bottom completed the message.

A Visual War

People found the widest variety of humor about the war in the same place they did the news, in magazines and newspapers. War news and commentary dominated their pages, understandably, but humor gave another perspective, a comic counterpoint to and relief from the serious dispatches and sober editorials. North and South, humor represented a laughably incompetent, rag-tag enemy whose corrupt principles were embodied in a degenerate and craven president. Scathing ridicule was also heaped upon enemies on the home front, shirkers of every stripe, and profiteers—anyone who put self-interest above the country's cause. It was the heyday of illustrated journalism, and publishers made the most of it. *Harper's Weekly* and *Leslie's Illustrated Newspaper*, the most popular magazines of the day, competed for readers with in-the-field artists who created crisply drawn, often full-page, illustrations of battles, fortifications, and camp life that gave visual authenticity to war-related stories. The same technology, needless to say, gave visual humor a significant place in the paper war. The dignified *Harper's Magazine*, subtitled "a Journal of Culture," put editorial cartoons on the last page but often included a warmly comic cover by Thomas Nast. Frank Leslie was not so high minded. A former engraver who had worked for P. T. Barnum, his publishing motto was "Never shoot over the reader's head," and he provided visual humor without apology, including double pages of multiple cartoon panels lampooning war-related foibles.[2] Before the war, *Harper's* and *Leslie's* had dominated the magazine market in the South, and as sectional tensions escalated they avoided alienating subscribers there; that changed with the fall of Fort Sumter, when they took a firm, pro-Union stance. It little mattered, though, not so much because the Union blockade would have prevented delivery, but with political independence, the antebellum argument for "a literature of our own" in the South took on new, pugnacious urgency. One response to the call was the *Southern Illustrated News* in 1862, a Confederate answer to *Harper's Magazine* and, like it, a "general" magazine that included humor. Unlike its Northern rival, though, illustrations were few and poorly rendered, given the want of engravers and suitable paper and ink.

Humor magazines founded in the North in the 1850s had been both challenged and inspired by the archetypal example of the London *Punch* (where the word "cartoon" originated) and made graphic humor a priority in the paper war. (In London, *Punch*, the *Comic News*, and *Fun* took a sardonically British stance.) *Yankee Notions* was well entrenched as war began, founded in 1852 by T. W. Strong, an engraver and publisher of comic valentines and illustrated "specials," as he called them. Frank Leslie added *Frank Leslie's Budget of Fun* to his publishing stable in 1859, the same year that *Phunny Phellow* and the *Comic Monthly* began publication.

The foremost humor magazine of the era, and the true American counterpart to *Punch*, was *Vanity Fair*, a New York weekly begun in December 1859. Like *Punch*, and unlike contemporaries at home, *Vanity Fair* had a sharp political edge and, with weekly publication, had a kind of continuity and timely relevance that its monthly rivals could not provide. Politically, it satirized "Copperhead" Peace Democrats, but the publishers *were* War Democrats and took on Lincoln and more radical Republicans as well. *Vanity Fair* was also more literary than its contemporaries, with occasional contributions from the likes of Thomas Bailey Aldrich, John Saxe, and William Dean Howells. Regular features included the burlesque war correspondence of George Arnold's "McArone" and Matthew Whittier's "Ethan Spike" letters. Looming large, then and now, was Charles Farrar Browne, as "Artemus Ward," the most popular humorist of the day, North and South, who edited *Vanity Fair* for a time and published his popular letters there. Visual humor was in the hands of one of the founders of the magazine, H. L. Stephens, who served as art editor, drew many of the cartoons, and employed the major illustrators and engravers of the day. *Vanity Fair* folded in May 1863, blaming a shortage of paper, but editorial turnover and its razor-sharp satire were more likely causes.

The Confederacy had nothing comparable when Fort Sumter fell, and while no one there seems to have called for "a humor of our own,"

"The Way Lincoln Will Be Lifted out of Washington City by
General Lee." From *Southern Punch* (30 April 1864).

war with the North inspired an appropriate response. The *Bugle Horn
of Liberty* had a spirited and ambitious agenda, caricaturing Lincoln,
specifically, and the North, broadly; publishing the letters of Bill Arp
(the Confederate answer to Artemus Ward); and skewering draft evad-
ers and "extortioners" on the home front. The vicissitudes of war
caught up with the *Bugle Horn of Liberty* all too soon, though; when its
offices in Griffin, Georgia, were taken over for a temporary hospital,
the publication folded in October 1863 after three issues.

Founded in August of the same year in Richmond, Virginia, the
relatively stable political and intellectual heart of the Confederacy,
the weekly *Southern Punch* survived to early 1865. As the title makes
clear, it was modeled on the London example, but implicitly it was
also the Confederate answer to *Vanity Fair*. The Union came in for its
fair share of comic derision, of course, but *Southern Punch* also took
an unrelentingly satiric look at foibles at home, such as pettifogging
politicians, a failing economy, and incompetent generals. "Serious"

writing—sketches of Southern political and military leaders and notices of Richmond theater performances—assured that a Confederate culture was alive and well. The lively spirit of *Southern Punch* never faltered, but over the months, the declining quality of paper, smaller type, narrower columns, smaller pages, and brief suspensions of publication silently testified to a nation enervated by war.

True to the London and New York examples, *Southern Punch* gave visual humor its due but suffered the lack of suitable engraving and printing endemic to Confederate publications. One cartoon (30 April 1864), therefore, would have been a pleasant surprise. Readers would have much enjoyed the delineation of the Union president routed out of the Union capitol on Confederate bayonets, even knowing that General in Chief of the Armies of the United States Ulysses S. Grant was grinding inexorably south to the Confederate capitol in April 1864. Only John Overall, editor of and chief contributor to *Southern Punch*, would have known that the cartoon had appeared before the war had begun, in *Frank Leslie's Budget of Fun* (15 March 1861). There, and then, the caption spoke to the dilemma of a recently inaugurated president bedeviled by those in the North who wanted him to declare war: "Oh, it's all well enough to say I must support by force the dignity of the high office you have elected me to—but it's darned uncomfortable sitting, I can tell yer!" For the Richmond editor in 1864, the pirated picture provided not only a much needed, nicely executed cartoon, but one that could be used for an inside joke on the consequences of Lincoln's ultimate decision to take on the Confederacy. With publishing centers far from battlefields and the necessities for printing virtually unlimited, the Union had what it needed to win the paper war, but not every battle.

Chapter One

HUMOR AND THE CIVIL WAR PRESIDENTS

Prologue: Defining the Enemy, Cavaliers and Yankees

The most fundamental purpose of humor in any war is to define the enemy, to put him in his comic, satiric place and thus make him and the cause he stands for laughable. With this war, that had to be done rather quickly because despite a long history of differences, real and even more strongly felt, the fall of Fort Sumter in April 1861 abruptly and dramatically altered the way they would be dealt with: even felt differences had to be made more real. Bluntly put, the ultimate purpose of the rhetoric of any war generally is to justify killing people, a principle all the more troublesome in this conflict because those "people" were in so many cases and so immediately, and often literally, "family." That war of words could take the form of highly original vituperation brought on for the occasion, as in the following stanzas from the anti-Union song sheet "Mayor Brown" (William Brown, of Baltimore):

> Then you puss-gut bolly-woppers,
> Mischief-makers through the town,
> You'll be put in mahogany garments,
> That is, when your [sic] done up brown.
>
> Oh! You fat enchanted maggots,
> Hypocrites of the Hicks degree, [Maryland governor
>   Thomas H. Hicks]

White-washed faces, bunch of faggots,
Lincoln hounds of misery.

This is early in the war, published shortly after the fall of Fort Sumter, and over the following years, a canonical vocabulary of ridicule and vituperation in the war of words would evolve. The first two paragraphs from "The Situation. As Viewed from Two Stumps" in *Yankee Notions* (March 1865) is a tour-de-force in that regard.

First Voice (*from the Northern stump*).—The men of the South are men of Belial, full of iniquity, hard of heart, and without bowels. Yes, they belong to the congregation of the ungodly, and meditate evil against Yankeedom, from the rising of the sun even to the going down of the same—from the first "eye-opener" before breakfast, to the last nip of hot brandy punch.

Second Voice (*from the Southern stump*).—The men of the North are the scum and offscourings of creation; abolitionists and wooly-heads; miscegenationists and nigger-worshippers; growers of onions and pedlars of wooden nutmegs; a nation of hucksters and cheats, of sniffling hypocrites and psalm-singing cowards. Their souls are no bigger than mustard seeds. Verily they are an abomination in our sight, and a stench in our nostrils! . . .

First Voice: Lo, the rebels are a ragged and seedy generation; their breeches are tattered; their toes stick out through their old boots. There is wailing and sadness among the chivalry. The day of their calamity has come upon them, and their cotton is a vain thing. No longer they flourish their bowie-knives and rattle their revolvers; no longer they burn with strong drink and brag and swear at horse-races and enjoying themselves in free fights around their court-houses.

Second Voice: Listen, all ye cowardly Yankees, and give ear to the truth! Four years you have fought to subjugate us; your fleets cover the sea and your armies fill the land; and still you imagine a vain thing. Have ye not learned that the Chivalry of the land of the Palm can never be conquered by cobblers of shoes, menders of eight-day clocks, and venders of rat-traps—by a nation that defile their hands with base labor, and peddle tin-ware an wooden milk-pails—that sing psalms through their noses and keep Thanksgiving!

This appeared in a New York humor magazine, and the "Northern stump" has both the first and the last word, but the Southern argument is no less unrelenting in the catalogue of invective so excessive that, appearing late in the war, it becomes a comically absurd apotheosis of the war of words.

A more generally applicable vocabulary prevailed that more effectively conceptualized the foe in the public discourse and the popular mindset. This takes its simplest, most immediate form in the terms commonly used to identify enemy soldiers. In the Civil War, Northerners were denounced as "invaders" and "vandals," Southerners as "traitors" and "rebels." Other terms spoke more descriptively to the historic cultural issues of the conflict. Southerners, for example, used "mudsills" (the bottom-most timber or "sill" of a building) to dismiss Northerners as uncouth, bottom-feeding wage slaves, which played to the implicit (at times explicit) contrast to what Confederate propaganda portrayed as a more benign form of Southern labor, slavery. Equivalents commonly used in Union popular literature would be "Southrons," a derisive tweaking of the word "Southerners," and "Secesh," a dismissive back-formation of "secessionist." While these terms were used derisively, each side willfully appropriated them at times to define themselves, a pugnacious way of showing, perhaps, that mere names would never harm them. Confederates, for example, often embraced the term "rebel" as a way of identifying with the winning side in the civil war of 1776. On the Union side, "The Mudsills Are Coming" was "sung with great applause" at a Boston opera house and extols the distinction between lowly mudsills and would-be aristocrats.

> The Union, the Union we're called on to save,
> Fall in the ranks to join our brothers brave;
> Chivalry, Chivalry, Old Abe's not a funning,
> For six hundred thousand Mudsills are coming.
> Now up, up, my boys, and be tramping along;
> We ne'er will return till the victory's won;
> We come from the mountains, the dells, and the hills,
> To show Southern Chivalry Northern Mudsills.

Success in battle made that distinction all the more sweet. Union troops occupying Yazoo City, Mississippi, in 1863 celebrated their victory with the *Yazoo Daily Yankee*, a newspaper published by "Mr. Mudsill, Mr. Small-Fisted Farmer, Mr. Greasy Mechanic & Co."

Two other terms, though, were used in the rhetoric of the time with broader meaning and relevance to designate the enemy as well as one's own partisans: "Cavalier" and "Yankee." Both had antebellum roots in the American experience, and by 1850, William R. Taylor writes in *Cavalier and Yankee*, they "expressed in the popular imagination the basic cultural conflict which people felt had grown up between a decorous, Agrarian South and the rootless, shifting, money-minded North" (1961, 335). The distinction was more perceived than real—"felt," as Taylor says—but war engenders propaganda that simplifies and amplifies the realities of history and the niceties of language.

The word "Yankee" originated in the Revolutionary War with English soldiers who used it to designate and denigrate the colonial foe. With what it would be easy to call "Yankee ingenuity," Americans took the sting out by adopting it as their own, and as "Jonathan" or "Brother Jonathan" and decked out in the iconic waistcoat and striped trousers, the rustic Yankee proliferated on stage and in poems, stories, and cartoons as the archetypal American. Not a designation that all Americans were comfortable with, for sure, even before 1861. To Southerners, the "Yankee" meant New Englanders who had duped them in horse deals, played cunning tricks, and peddled fake nutmegs, wooden hams, rifle flints made of horn, and more. Given unflagging English disparagement of Americans, though, "even the Georgian does not hesitate to call himself a Yankee," James Fenimore Cooper wrote in *Notions of the Americans*. "The Americans are particularly fond of distinguishing anything connected with their general enterprise, skill, or reputation by this term" (quoted in Nickels 1993, 13–16).

That was in 1828, but regional differences hardened over the next three decades, and any semblance of a "universal Yankee nation," as the popular antebellum phrase had it, ended with gunfire at Fort Sumter in 1861. An 1862 lithograph titled "Yankee Volunteers Marching into Dixie" (see plate 1) makes the break graphically clear with endless ranks of armed, look-alike Brother Jonathans headed south.

For a South at war, now the Confederate States of America, "Yankee" meant much more than clever peddlers and tricksters of prewar popular culture, although such labels continued as convenient, vestigial libels. The South could now be "free from the thralls of Yankee-diddle-daddle-doodledom," as George Bagby put it in 1861 (quoted in Faust 1988, 38), and that meant everything from language (spelling, pronunciation, and vocabulary) to a host of radical innovations that clearly distinguished the values of the two regions. A *Southern Punch* editorial (22 August 1862) catalogued them as "the diabolisms of Free Love, Women's Rights, Abolitionism and the lesser 'isms' of this wicked race." In the North, antislavery zealots were a distinct and unpopular minority in the North, but for Confederate propaganda, abolitionism was the sine quo non of Yankee perfidy. During the war, "Yankee," in other words, connoted an array of associative implications from suspicion to outright contempt. In much of the South, it still does.

In the South, "Cavalier" stood for everything the North was not, an ethos that meant a distinct and superior moral and racial alternative to the materialistic, ethnically and turbulently urban, fanatical North—again, vices summed up in one word, "Yankee." It was a culture sanctioned in the Waverly novels of Sir Walter Scott so popular in the South, as well as antebellum "plantation" novels, and had much to do with the formation of the myth of the "Lost Cause" after 1865. Historically, if inaccurately, Confederate writers rooted their identity in the seventeenth-century English Cavaliers and their war with the English Puritans. The Cavaliers did lose that one, but looking back to the eleventh-century Norman knights, they did defeat the Saxons, ancestors of the present-day Puritans, according to this Confederate reading of the past. A Louisville, Kentucky, editor succinctly brought it all together and up to date in 1862: "The Norman cavalier of the South cannot brook the vulgar familiarity of the Saxon Yankee" (quoted in Osterweis 1949, 101).

For Union propagandists, "Cavalier," embodied too in the word "chivalry," made for a characterization easily satirized. Also identified as an "F. F. V." (First Families of Virginia) or just "F. F.," since not only Virginians were blameworthy, the Cavalier was lampooned as indolent, effete, and self-indulgent, a way of life made possible by slave labor. Painting all Southerners as slave-beating, Cavalier planters was no more realistic than the Confederate indictment of all Northerners as avid abolitionists, but they were both potent images in the popular mind. Robert H. Newell's poem "South Carolina Gentleman," published in various forms and performed on stage, wrings every drop from the Cavalier caricature.

> Down in a small Palmetto State the curious ones may find,
> A ripping, tearing gentleman of an uncommon kind,
> A staggering, swaggering sort of chap who takes his whiskey
> straight.

Newell misses nothing amiss. This "Gentleman" dresses lavishly but without taste, carries a bowie-knife and a pistol, "chews tobacco by the pound and spits upon the floor," gambles compulsively and cheats. Unsparing, certainly, but Newell goes further with a libel, usually unspoken publicly, that gives the ultimate lie to Confederate pretensions to racial superiority.

> You trace his genealogy, and not far back you'll see,
> A most undoubted Octoroon or mayhap a mustee,
> And if you note the shaggy locks that cluster on his brow,
> You'll find that every other hair is varied with a kink that
>   seldom denotes pure Caucasian blood, but on the contrary
>   betrays an admixture with a race not particularly popular
>   now:
> This South Carolina gentleman, one of the present time.

A broadside version says "as sung by J. C. Cross," and the irony would have been heightened by a performance before a theater audience if Cross did so in his persona as "the favorite Ethiopian Comedian."

The stereotypes of the Cavalier and Yankee had roots in antebellum America; with war they became the basis for defining an enemy not to be feared, the embodiment of the nation and culture he defended, one who could be killed without compunction. A Union pictorial envelope did it all in the satirical delineation of "a Southern Gorilla," a disheveled, unkempt "knight" bristling with weapons, cheap whiskey at the

"A Southern Gorilla (Guerilla)." Courtesy of the Collection of the New-York Historical Society.

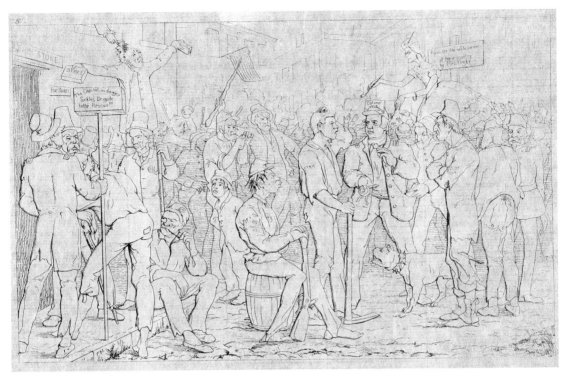

"Enlistment of Sickles's Brigade."
Courtesy of Special Collections,
University of Virginia Library.

ready, a whip for slaves. The poem, by Robert Newell, details the corrupt principles he fights for.

The work of German-born Baltimore dentist, artist, and Confederate activist Adalbert Volck was privately published, but his skillfully executed sketches accurately captured Confederate popular thinking. "Enlistment of Sickles's Brigade," from *Sketches from the Civil War of North America* (1863), draws a stark picture of Daniel Sickles's recruiting a brigade in New York City, with visual references to specifics of that event in May 1861: Bibles and pipes reportedly given as recruiting inducements appear in the background. Volck's tableau of an unkempt mob of lowlifes gathered outside a saloon—surly Irish and bewhiskered "Hessians" dominate the street scene—is the graphic incarnation of a mongrel Northern society. (In fact, though, Sickles's "Excelsior Brigade" did turn out to be unruly soldiers.) To Volck, the Union recruits "were mostly from the very dregs of the people and it was not without

CASTLE LINCOLN—NO SURRENDER!   FORT DAVIS—IN RUINS!!

"Castle Lincoln—No Surrender!
Fort Davis—In Ruins!" Courtesy
of the American Antiquarian
Society.

cause that the South complained that they had to fight the scum of the
earth" (Voss 1988, 74). The lines were drawn in the paper war.

The Presidents

In the rhetoric of war that leads to and then justifies armed conflict,
the leader of the enemy becomes the living embodiment of everything
wrong with the other side. This is a strategy well suited to a civil war
because the people are "one of us" and not so much adversaries but
victims of a deluded, even deranged, leader: the war becomes "personal" with that person only. To look at an earlier civil war, the opening
words of "The Declaration of Independence" of July 4, 1776—"When
in the course of human events"—have been invoked annually for over
two hundred years; but for the purposes of that time, a catalogue of
the many transgressions of King George III dominates that declaration and the war propaganda it engendered. Also, humorous and
satirical attacks upon a particular person cut through abstract philo-
sophical discourse and create striking verbal and pictorial images that

"One of the F. F. V.'s Colonel of the Dysentery Blues who thinks his martial appearance will strike terror into the hearts of the 'Northern Mudsills.'" Courtesy of the Collection of the New-York Historical Society.

become a convenient, shorthand vocabulary easily reiterated in the varied texts of popular culture. Both Jefferson Davis and Abraham Lincoln, for example, were portrayed repeatedly as drunks, wannabe kings, and in league with the devil (at times all three at once), personal attacks meant to discredit the political and social agendas for which they purportedly stood.

It is also a strategy that puts a "face," even literally, on the abstractions generated by war propaganda. Although he is not named in the caption, the face of Jefferson Davis appears on a pictorial envelope lampooning the aristocratic, Cavalier posturing of the Confederate enemy. As for Lincoln in Confederate satire, the title of a story in *Southern Punch* (21 January 1864) called him the "King of the Yankees," who willfully and willingly admits, "The rebels call me a Gorilla. Be it so. I *am* a Gorilla ruling a wilderness of monkeys who laugh and chatter and do my bidding. I am master of the Yankee menagerie."

Even latter-day, kindly disposed biographers call Jefferson Davis "stern" and "humorless," whereas throughout his political life Lincoln was well known, even notorious, as we will see, for his humor. His appearance too—the beard, his height, his craggy face—loomed large in popular humor. Not so the Confederate president. According to the *Natchez Daily Courier* (13 May 1863), "the correspondent of the *Charleston Mercury,* says the following story, is current in Richmond":

> In the Capitol Square, a few days ago, a drunken soldier accosted the President:
> "Are you Mr. Davis?"
> "I am," was the stern reply.
> "Are you the President of the Confederate States?"
> "I am."
> "Well, I thought you looked like a postage stamp."

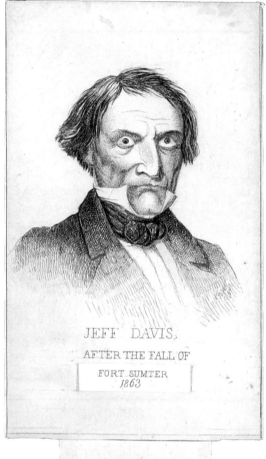

"Jeff Davis after the Fall of . . ."
Two views of one metamorphic.
Courtesy of Special Collections
Research Center, Syracuse
University Library.

The classical, chiseled face of Jefferson Davis did appear on Confederate stamps, and this anecdote pretty much sums up the good humor to be had at the expense of Davis in the South. (Most presidential decisions, though, provoked excoriations aplenty.) He says only two stern words, but they are one with the notion that he looks like, belongs on, a postage stamp. The brief story pokes some gentle fun at the president (his patrician face), but implicitly it affirms the truth of that characterization.

That profile was well known in the North too, where there were no qualms about caricaturing the Confederate president without let or hindrance, and no lack of resources for doing so in any number of elaborate and inventive ways, as in a unique "metamorphic." Moving the tab in the "pocket" dramatically alters the president's reaction to the reversal of Confederate fortunes represented in the "window" at the bottom. Although anti-Davis propaganda, it is also a commodity, one that could be modified and sold again: another version used the fall of Vicksburg (May 1863) as the occasion for the change of expression.

Illustrated envelopes were a much less expensive commodity, and thousands were printed, with engravers making the most of the limited space available to create over 250 visual caricatures of Davis as the living embodiment of Confederate perfidy. A common strategy was to put a realistic face on a non-human body, most often a dog. In "Secession Web" (see plate 2) Davis appears as a spider trapping unsuspecting flies (states) into his "secession web." The skull and crossbones on his back appeared initially to portray Davis and cohorts as pirates and then became a more general visual clue for the death and destruction that his regime foreboded.

Illustrated envelopes also took on more elaborate forms, as in a collectable series of camp views, battles scenes, and military buildings that covered the front of the envelope. A humorous series of this kind published in 1861 delineates five rounds of a boxing match between the two presidents. In "3rd Round," Lincoln has humiliated Davis by tearing off a hunk of his trousers, forcing General Beauregard and the rest of the presidential entourage to retreat to Richmond.

As president, Davis also represented the Confederacy incarnate in many cartoons published in the illustrated weeklies. "Columbia Awake at Last," in *Harper's Weekly* (8 June 1861), divides thematically into two vertical parts. On the right, in the background, the spirit of George Washington looks on with benign approval as the Union, represented by the boldly drawn, Amazon-like Columbia, protects the Constitution

"Lincoln: I Will Soon Smother Those Pirates." Courtesy of the Collection of the New-York Historical Society.

with one hand and with the other reaches into the Confederate half of the picture to throttle Jefferson Davis. There, caricature prevails, with a clownish, bug-eyed Davis, who cannot stand on his spindly legs, labeled "secession" and "treason." The muscular arm of Lady Liberty has shaken loose a hidden knife, derringer, and bottle of whiskey, icons of the "real" Chivalry, as are the Confederate flag and a Palmetto tree (symbol of South Carolina, the first state to secede) stuck in his Cavalier-like hat. Behind Davis one of his craven companions also sports the tree, the other a pirate flag.

◊ ◊ ◊

Visually striking as they are, graphic presentations are essentially static: what you see is what you get; other genres used much the same motifs and themes, combining them with narrative and the characterizations those genres make possible. In the widely printed song sheet "Jeff Davis," sung to "Nell Flaugherty's Drake," an Irishman heaps abuse on the Confederate president as responsible for his recent tough luck.

> Once I could eat my fill of good meat,
> And whiskey galore I could roule into me;
> I could stroll up and down every street in this town,
> With always a quarter to go on a spree.

COLUMBIA AWAKE AT LAST.

"Columbia Awake at Last."
Courtesy of Special Collections/
Musselman Library, Gettysburg
College.

My clothes they were good, I ne'er thought of wood,
A pig or a spade never entered my mind;
But now I'm in grief, since the black-hearted thief,
Jeff Davis, he brought these hard times unto me!

The chorus alludes to Davis as a traitor but, like the verses, is personal
and comic.

Bad luck to him early! bad luck to him dearly!
May the devil admire him where'er he may be!
May Mosquitoes bite him, and Rattle-snakes smite him,
The Traitor that brought these hard times unto me!

"Paddy's" way to even the score is as personal as his complaint:

I'll spit in my fist, and then I'll enlist,
And off to the wars I'd march bould as brass;
I'll fight till I die and ne'er will I fly,
I'll measure the length of myself on the grass:
Like a Brigadier-private I'll rush on the foe,
And I'll lather the Rebels both high and low
It's then I'll knock blazes, out of Jefferson Davis,
The vile traitor that brought these hard times unto me!

Davis comes off more comical than satirical because so much of the
intended humor is in the stereotypical, comic (albeit here, patriotic)
Irishman, second only to the African American as a popular theater

"Judas Vile Betrayed His Master . . ." Courtesy of the Collection of the New-York Historical Society.

caricature; and what with the "brogue" and the topical allusions, the piece most surely originated on stage.

The significant (and for that reason highly complex) place of the African American characterization in Civil War humor needs the separate chapter it has in this book, but a look into that related place in regard to Jefferson Davis, and to Abraham Lincoln as well, is appropriate here. In the song sheet "Jeff Davis' Lament," the Confederate president longs to be back home in Mississippi, far from the economic and military wreck he admits he has made of the Confederacy.

> In de cotton state ob ole Mis-sip-py,
> I libbed from day to day,
> A payin my debts by pudiation,
> Which am a berry nice way.
> But now I'se got to de border states,
> And de money is most run ashore;
> Oh I wish I'se back in ole Missippy,
> I'd nebber come here any more.
>
> If I was dar and at my ease,
> I'd nebber come dis way;
> I'd let ole Abe do jist as he please,
> And at my home I'd stay.
> For here in Virginny he holds me tight,
> While de Hatteras guns do roar;
> Oh do lemme go to ole Missippy,
> I'll nebber come back any more.
>
> I spect we'll get cotched, and de next we'll know,
> We'll dangle side by side;
> And de people will say I libbed like a fool,
> And like a fool I died.
> So now jist stay in de cotton fields,
> And nebber come north to war,
> Or else you'll get hung like I shall be here,
> And nebber get back any more.

That Davis himself admits to the errors of his ways was a popular satirical strategy (Lincoln does it too in Confederate satire), but that he does so in the blackface minstrel dialect of the original air, "Carry Me to Old Virginia Shore," magnifies the humiliation. An illustrated

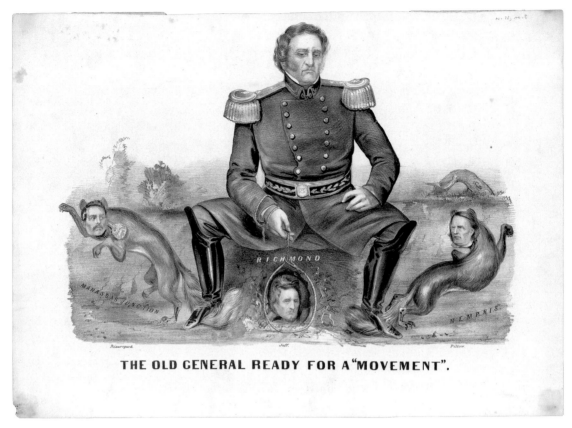

THE OLD GENERAL READY FOR A "MOVEMENT".

"The Old General Ready for a
'Movement.'" Courtesy of the
American Antiquarian Society.

envelope rubs it in visually. Davis as consummate traitor was the most
common indictment, and here he admits to treason equal to Judas's,
but the humor is in the figure of the newly freed slave, his chains now
attached to the rope that strings up "traitor Davis," as he was often
called. It all adds to the indignity of the Confederate president but has
nothing to do with the slave's freedom.

Making Davis the enemy incarnate and scapegoat for Confederate
sins justified treating him in ways that pushed the boundaries of taste
of the time. The broadside "Ballad of the Great Fight; Between the
Union Eagle and the Old Rooster, Jeff. Davis" puts the war in terms of
a battle between the generalized "Union Eagle" and the more person-
alized Jefferson Davis as the "Old Rooster."[1]

> Of all the fighting fowls I know,
> The Eagle is the scrouger;

He's got a nail on every toe
That fits him for a gouger.
There is a little Southern cock,
Jeff. Davis is that rooster's name,
His crowing threatens dangers,
But though he tries to pass for game,
He's but a dung-hill ranger.
Come Rooster Jeff, put on your gaffs
And fix yourself for action;
Our fowl will be afoul of you
And give you satisfaction.

The apparently innocent use of "dung" and "afoul" in the early stanzas sets up the more explicit scatology in what follows.

The way he'll claw you fore and aft,
Oh Jeff, will make you flutter,
Your bowels will dissolve with fear
And run like melted butter.
You'll find yourself in nasty plight
Before this work is ended,
And with the fume that you produce
Each nose will be offended.
Our Eagle, when he smells you, Jeff,
Will swear you stink with knavery,
And think that Buzzards ought to eat
A carcass so unsavory.

Doggerel dirty work here; the popular printmakers Currier and Ives were more allegorically subtle with their 1861 lithograph "The Old General Ready for a 'Movement.'" Looking much younger than his seventy-five years, General in Chief of the Union Army Winfield Scott squats on a mound labeled "Richmond," holding a noose, waiting for Davis to "move" into it. (The face is, in fact, that of Confederate General Gideon Pillow.) Although Scott is fully dressed, his pose and the quotation marks around the word "Movement" in the title suggest it is not a military evacuation he is ready for.

That the Confederate president needed or deserved a "physic" or "cathartic" became another way to suggest the scatological motif, as in an illustrated envelope that portrays Lincoln as a pharmacist very well prepared to "doctor" the Confederacy in a variety of ways (see plate 3).

"Finale of the 'Jeff Davis Die-Nasty.'" Courtesy of the Library of Congress.

The broadside "The Great Union War Song, 'Physic for Traitors'" has more to say about how rebels should be "treated," concluding with hemp as the "herb" most appropriate—here, the rope for traitors.

> Say, who are the bold agitators
> That dare to get up such a row?
> Let us hunt up the rascally Traitors
> And thoroughly physic them now,
> And thoroughly physic them now.
> Let us hunt up the rascally Traitors,
> And thoroughly physic them now.
>
> We'll doctor them all in short metre,
> And give the dogs physic enough;
> Charcoal, brimstone, well mix'd with salt petre,
> And lead pills are the right sort of stuff.
> But take notice, ye Union haters,
> It's a fact, by the Doctors confess'd,
> That of all kinds of Physic for Traitors,
> Pure Hemp is the finest and best.

"Jeff Davis Caught at Last, Hoop Skirts and Southern Chivalry." Courtesy of the American Antiquarian Society.

That herb well deserves cultivation,
Oh scatter its seed all around,—
Let it flourish in every plantation,
While Rebels and Traitors abound.
Down, down with the tyrant "King Cotton,"
King Hemp holds the rascal in check.
If you can't cure the heart that's all rotten,
Try a bandage of Hemp on the neck.

The climax of satiric fun at Davis's expense came at the end of the war with the story that, having escaped from Richmond, he had been captured in Georgia on 10 May 1865, disguised in his wife's clothing. According to his own account, in his haste he had mistakenly put on a raglan that belonged to his wife, who had also, thoughtfully, thrown a shawl over his shoulders.[2] Whatever the truth, in the months that followed, the story lead to an extraordinary number and variety of humorous versions—stories, poems, songs, broadsides, *cartes-de-visites,* and at least two illustrated comic books—that portrayed him as "The Shero," "Jeff in Petticoats," and "The Belle of Richmond." The earliest newspaper stories connected his capture with rounding up the culprits involved in the assassination of Lincoln less than a month earlier, and the subsequent outrageous representations of the demise of the Confederate president provided a kind of parallel comic catharsis to the ongoing mourning. A lithograph published soon after the capture evokes a wide range of emotional responses. The top half is a somber allegorical version of Lincoln's death, titled "Freedom's Immortal Triumph!" where, from left to right, "Justice," Lady Liberty, and angels escort the dead president to heaven. That idealism contrasts with the grimly humorous, but even more stylized, "realistically" detailed bottom half, titled with the crude pun, "Finale of the 'Jeff Davis Die-Nasty.'" In contrast to the allegorically idealized femininity above, we have Jeff Davis below in hoopskirts and boots, knife in one hand, tattered Confederate flag in the other, hanging from a sour apple tree, long an icon in popular culture for his ultimate fate. Lined up to the right for the same fate here, with Robert E. Lee leading the van, are other Confederate traitors awaiting their destiny—coconspirators in Lincoln's assassination in the minds of many at the time, a suspicion confirmed with the figure of John Wilkes Booth, pistol in hand, rushing up to take his rightful place. Completing the picture of presidential perfidy in the background are reminders of the Confederacy's most infamous prisons, Libby, in Richmond, and Andersonville, Georgia, not far from where Davis was captured.

Certain icons quickly became the "language" in popular culture for retelling his capture in broadsides, cartoons, sheet music, and the like: that he was dressed in a *hoopskirt*; that he tried to escape under the pretense of going for a *bucket* of water; that his *boots* exposed the ruse; that he had brandished a *knife*; and that he was absconding with Confederate *gold*. Most of these can be seen in the 1865 lithograph "Jeff Davis Caught at Last. Hoop Skirts and Southern Chivalry."

The one icon that dominates the interpretative spin on Davis's capture from the beginning and in all genres is his being dressed in

Carte-de-visite of Davis
in wife's clothes. From the
collection of the author.

women's clothing, an image that became fixed as a crinoline petticoat. Also called a hoopskirt, or a balmoral, it had long been a potent symbol of femininity in the popular imagination. The immediate comic response today is to the incongruity of Jefferson Davis in drag, but in 1865 it represented the ultimate critique of the Cavalier myth that the Confederacy had fought to defend. It gave the lie to Southern leaders, Nina Silber concludes, "who had boasted of their more civilized society, their greater concern for the weaker sex, their military prowess, and their manly courage." Thus, "a blow aimed at Jefferson Davis's manliness also targeted the class pretenses of the southern 'chivalry'" (Silber 1993, 33). Punctuated by its terse caption, the lithograph "Jefferson Davis. Caught at Last. Hoop Skirts and Southern Chivalry" makes that connection visually clear. The last stanza of the song sheet "Capture of Jeff. Davis" has much the same message but with a significantly different messenger.

> Now there's your Southern chivalry, to hide in a woman's
> dress;

It shows he was an old fool, or he'd took off his boots, I
  guess;
De rebels dey did blow how de Yankees dey would switch;
But in a woman's dress, is a queer place for the last ditch.

On the printed page, the black dialect contributes its ironic effect to
the demise of Confederate chivalry, but performed on stage, as this
piece was, would have made for visual and aural additions to the
humiliation.

An invention of popular culture in the first place, the affair became
increasingly exploited for reasons that had little to do with Jefferson
Davis or the Confederacy. A cartoon pamphlet titled "The Life of Jeff
Davis," for example, used it to lampoon the women's movement, calling Davis a "Bloomer," the mode of dress promoted by feminist Ame-
lia Bloomer. "A change of UNIFORM is necessary. He now believes in
WOMEN'S RIGHTS and avails himself of the advantage." The affair
quickly became a commodity, turned into merchandise for sale, giving
ironic credence to the Confederate libel of all Northerners as money-
grubbing Yankees. The "facts" of the capture leant themselves well
to visual embellishments, and given the technology of the time the
results could be mass produced and thus bought cheaply. Over two
dozen *cartes-de-visites* alone were marketed, most of them crude versions of previously published engravings. (Like other cartes-de-visites,
some were stamped "Sold by a One Armed Soldier" on the back.) More
creative is an apparent photograph of Davis in a formal gown and
holding the pair of boots that reportedly exposed his disguise. It is, in
fact, a doctored carte-de-visite of his wife, Varina, and they were sold
as a pair, hers with "Mrs. Jeff Davis" on the back, his with "Jeff Davis
Herself."

P. T. Barnum turned it all into the ultimate show, but not of patriotism. Failing to buy the clothing the Confederate president had been
captured in, he had a wax figure made, labeled it "The Belle of Richmond," and it appeared as the highlight of the attractions at his American Museum in New York. Shortly after, 13 July 1865, fire engulfed the
building, creating a "scene of terror" that was "not without its comic
incidents," the *New York Times* reported the next day. A man trying to
rescue the effigy of Davis "fought vigorously to preserve the worthless
thing, as though it were a gem of rare value," but to no avail.

On reaching the balcony the man, perceiving that either the inan-
imate Jeff. or himself must go by the board, hurled the scarecrow

to the iconoclasts in the street. As Jeff. made his perilous descent, his petticoats again played him false, and as the wind blew them about, the imposture of the figure was exposed. The flight of dummy Jeff. was the cause of great merriment among the multitude, who saluted the queer-looking thing with cheers and uncontrollable laughter.

Barnum, the consummate Yankee, had it replaced.

◊ ◊ ◊

Abraham Lincoln was damned and ridiculed by the Confederacy even before he was sworn in as president. In *The Image of Lincoln in the South*, Michael Davis gives a good sense of that treatment in summing up and quoting Southern editorial judgments of the newly elected president: "He was 'the leanest, lankest, most ungainly mass of legs and arms and hatchet face ever strung on a human frame,'" . . . "a horrid looking wretch . . . sooty and scoundrelly [*sic*] in aspect, a cross between the nutmeg dealer, the horse swapper, and the night man.'" In short, as Davis concludes, he was "the very antithesis of the Cavalier ideal" (1971, 14–15). And as a consequence, in short again, Lincoln was the very "thesis" of the hated Yankee trickster of antebellum popular literature—"the nutmeg dealer, the horse swapper"—despite his Southern origins (like Jefferson Davis, he was born in Kentucky) and his Western (Illinois) background. (This was in 1860, and nothing changed in four years: "Lincoln alone harmonizes in himself all of those qualities which are essential to a representation of average Yankeeism," the *Richmond Dispatch* [7 April 1864] concluded.) Even his looks, "ungainly" and "horrid," contrasted unfavorably to the patrician profile of the Confederate president. (But Lincoln would also appear on postage stamps.) As for his being a "night man," one who empties privies at night, it is an obscure allusion, but typical of the catch-all slanders both presidents endured.

Most telling here is the word "sooty," a crude swipe, but one of the more subtle allusions to Lincoln's having "Negro" blood, the supposedly factual cornerstone for the accusation that he was an abolitionist, the leader of what were called the radical "Black Republicans." Less subtle epithets in publications and private correspondence included "Ape-raham," "Ape Lincoln," "the Old Baboon," and "Abraham Africanus" in the 1864 book of the same name. (William Russell Smith's long poem, *The Royal Ape* (1863), did not play up that connection, but

Lincoln as a monkey. Courtesy
of the Lilly Library, Indiana
University, Bloomington, Indiana.

"The MacLincoln Harrisburg Highland Fling." Courtesy of the American Antiquarian Society.

Lincoln peering out of a train car.
Courtesy of Special Collections,
University of Virginia Library.

"The Abe-iad." Courtesy of the Abraham Lincoln Library and Museum of Lincoln Memorial University, Harrogate, Tennessee.

for some Confederate editors it went too far in suggesting sexual misconduct on the part of the First Family [Abel 2000, 102]). Lincoln's Emancipation Proclamation in 1863 was proof positive of his racial heritage. A cartoon published in Richmond that year showed a furry Lincoln with a baboon tail squatting on a Union flag, gleefully presenting the document to a delighted black.

As with Jefferson Davis, popular culture turned certain incidents into continual sources of laughter and ridicule; with the Union president it started early and close to home. In Harrisburg, Pennsylvania, on his way by train from Illinois to the Capitol for inauguration in 1861, aides warned him of an assassination plot by Baltimore gangs such as the Plug Uglies and Blood Tubs. Urged to take a different train through the city, he did—and here the tale begins—purportedly disguised in a military cape and/or Scottish cap. The incident was caricatured with fairly good humor in the North, as in "The MacLincoln Harrisburg Highland Fling" in *Vanity Fair* (9 March 1861). Confederate illustrator Adalbert Volck drew it up more satirically with his precise, realistic lines that belie his inaccurate portrayal of the Union president-elect hiding out in a boxcar. It is inaccurate, but artfully rendered, what with the cat's reaction that draws the viewer's eye to the president-to-be's bizarre costume, his craven gaze, and fearful posture. Visually, the incident played out fairly quickly, but in other forms it survived as a way to disparage his character in many satires both North and South.

The broadside "The Last Race of the Rail-Splitter," probably printed shortly after the Union defeat at First Manassas, refers to the incident as an early example of a cowardly president who played it safe in the White House, another common motif of anti-Lincoln satire, as was his being a drunk.

> He was so scar'd that dreary night,
> When hidden like a cask or bail,
> In railroad cars, from ev'ry sight,
> He pass'd this city on the rail.
>
> Said Old Abram, as is he,
> Soak'd with whiskey, or with rum,
> These city boys, are death to me,
> 'Tis safer hide and from them run.
>
> The night he hid, and sent his wife,
> Where dead next day she might be found,
> And lose, on Central Road, her life,
> Whilst hidden, he went dodging round.
>
> Said Old Abram, as was he,
> Soak'd with whiskey, or with rum,
> My wife is very good, you see,
> To die for me and let me run.

The sheet music "The Abe-iad," by "J. P. McRebel," circa 1861, brings together with vituperative glee the stock charges against the Union president—that he was the uncommonly ugly leader of a motley rabble, an abolitionist—all of it thrown in with the Baltimore incident, which provided a cartoon for the cover. *Southern Punch* (24 October 1863) revived the incident in the poem "Lincoln's Dream, A Reminiscence of the Past," compounding the slander this time with

Mrs. Lincoln's defiance of the city toughs in contrast to her husband's cowardice.

> He turned to Mrs. Lincoln then,
> This President, yet pig of men,
> "My dear!" said he, "I see them all,
> Each bloody, thugging cannibal."
> "How do they flourish?" then said she,
> "If I were a man, they couldn't scare me!
> Face them, and down with the reckless crew."
> "*You* may!" said he—"d—d if I do!"
> So he muffled up in a Scottish plaid
> And a regimental coat 'tis said—
> Cut out on the cars, with fright half dead,
> And left Mrs. L. snoring in bed.

At the end of the war, diehard Confederate sympathizers in the North charged that the story of Jefferson Davis's taking "refuge in his wife's petticoats [was] an abolition lie," one "manufactured by the 'radicals' as an offset to the Scotch cap and cloak story," reported the *Trenton (New Jersey) Daily State Gazette* (23 May 1865). A friend of Confederate diarist Mary Chesnut thought so too. Recalling "the manner of Lincoln and the Scotch cape that he hid his ugly face with," she concluded, "It is that escapade of their man Lincoln that set them [Yankees] on making up the waterproof cloak story of Jefferson Davis" (Chesnutt 1981, 819).

◊ ◊ ◊

Lincoln had to contend not only with serious divisions within his own party (some Republicans thought him too harsh on the South, others too lenient) but also with the opposition of Democrats and, above all, with Peace Democrats, or Copperheads, Confederate sympathizers who churned out anti-Lincoln literature more venomous than anything published in the South. And enemies in the North had the financial resources to vent: broadsides, lithograph cartoons, sheet music, and poems were printed by the thousands, along with joke books, campaign biographies, and songsters galore, all of them with a political axe to grind, satirical hay to make.

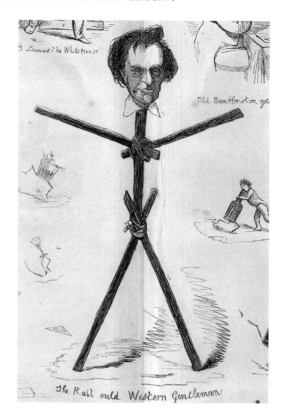

"The Rail Ould Western Gentleman." Reproduction by permission of the Buffalo & Erie County Public Library, Buffalo, New York.

The mainstream media in the North often treated Lincoln with tolerably good humor, although that changed in response to events as they unfolded, such as military success or failure, his announcement of the Emancipation Proclamation in September 1862, and the 1864 presidential election. Early on, he was portrayed as the lanky, rough-hewn common man from the West, the rail-splitter who knew the value of physical labor. "The Humors of the Presidential Canvass," in the *Comic Monthly* (August 1860), featured two pages of various cartoons of the four presidential candidates. The drawing of Lincoln humorously combines the iconic fence rails with his tall, slender frame and dominates the center of the piece. The result is not overtly unkind, but neither is it particularly dignified. Over the years, the iconic timber would be portrayed in a variety of editorial ways: a lever, a baseball bat, a spear, a balance beam, and more.

His distinctive physical appearance played some part in most characterizations, homey or homely, depending upon the political point of view. In anti-Lincoln satire, what he thought and did were every bit as grotesque as how he looked. As the title of Rev. E. P. Birch's broadside "The Devil's Visit to 'Old Abe'" suggests, the Union president is in league with the Devil and looks the part:

> His cheek bones were high and his visage was rough,
> Like a middling of bacon all wrinkled and tough;
> His nose was as long, and as ugly and big
> As the snout of a half-starved Illinois pig.

Satan takes credit for Lincoln's loathsome agenda and has done what he can to promote it:

> I stirred up the North with its vagabond crew,
> And set witch burning Yankeedom all in a stew.
> With its isms and schisms—fanatical trappings—
> Its free-loving humbugs, and spiritual trappings.

In the end, though, even the Devil is appalled at what Lincoln has wrought:

> I have tutored the world in lying and sinning,
> But it stirs my soul with grief and vexation
> To see your abominable Yankee nation
> Outstripping me far in the deaths of its shame,
> And heaping reproach on my kingdom and name.

All of this was inspired by Lincoln's proclamation—the one calling for prayer and fasting following the disaster at Manassas in July 1861.

By contrast, the description of Lincoln in a mock campaign biography got up for the hotly contested 1864 election, while hardly complimentary, is more facetious than mean spirited.

> Mr. Lincoln stands six feet twelve in his socks, which he changes once every ten days. His anatomy is composed mostly of bones, and when walking he resembles the offspring of a happy marriage between a derrick and a windmill. . . . His head is shaped something like a ruta-bago, and his complexion is that of a Saratoga trunk. His hands and feet are plenty large enough, and in society he has the air of having too many of them. . . . He can hardly be

768

Long ABRAHAM LINCOLN a Little Longer.

FISK & HATCH.

called handsome, though he is certainly much better looking since he had the small-pox. . . . He is 107 years old. (*Only Authentic Life* [1864], 14–15)

Lincoln did win the election, and artist Frank Bellew treated the occasion and Lincoln's lanky frame with some gentle verbal and visual humor in "Long Abraham Lincoln a Little Longer" in *Harper's Weekly* (26 November 1864). In retrospect, his assassination within five months makes the "little longer" pun tragically ironic in retrospect.

◊ ◊ ◊

Not only was Abraham Lincoln the subject of humor, but so was his reputation for joking. There were even jokes about his making jokes, and one made the rounds as "the best story he ever read in the papers of himself," according to the *San Antonio Daily Express* (6 July 1870).[3]

Two Quakeresses were traveling on the railroad and were heard discussing the probable determination of the war. "I think," said the first, "that Jefferson [Davis] will succeed." "Why does thee think so?" asked the other. "Because Jefferson is a praying man." "And so is Abraham [Lincoln] a praying man," objected the second. "Yes, but the Lord will think Abraham is joking," the first replied conclusively.

"Long Abraham Lincoln a Little Longer." Courtesy of Special Collections, University of Virginia Library.

Lincoln's reputation for joking stretched back to his early years as a country lawyer, but as Paul M. Zall writes in *Abe Lincoln Laughing*, "about sixty percent of the stories assigned to him during his lifetime can be linked to previously published sources" (1982, 3). His tales or not, many fostered an image of a wartime president whose humor entertained but was also a strategy to "repress idle curiosity without giving offence" and to "divert conversation from dangerous topics," as the *New Orleans Daily True Delta* (7 March 1864) wrote. Newspapers printed stories on the subject over the years and continued over the decades after his death, usually with the assurance that it was a good one—and true. "One of the best stories told of the President is as follows," reported the *San Francisco Bulletin* (11 March 1862):

A visitor at the White House asked him what number of men he supposed the rebels had in the field. The President responded, seriously, "1,200,000, according to the best authority." The interrogator, blanched in the face, ejaculated, "My God!" The President continued: "Yes, sir, 1,200,000—no doubt of it. You see, all our generals, when they get whipped, say the enemy outnumbers them from three to five to one, and I must believe them. We have 400,000 men in the field, and three times four make twelve. Don't you see it?"

Some versions pinned the anecdote down with "The inquisitive man looked for his hat not soon after 'seeing it.'"

The gist of one story like that earned a lasting place in the canon of Lincoln lore.

Like many of his peers, the distinguished conqueror of the Mississippi, Gen. Grant, has been charged with indulging in intoxicating drinks. A committee, just previous to the fall of Vicksburg, solicitous for the morale of our armies, took it upon themselves to visit the President and urge the removal of Gen. Grant. "For what?" said Mr. Lincoln. "Why, he drinks too much whisky." "Ah!" rejoined Mr. Lincoln, "can you inform me, gentlemen, where General Grant procures his whisky?" The "committee" confessed they could not. "Because," added Old Abe, with a merry twinkle in his eyes, "If I can find out, *I'll send every General in the field a barrel of it!*" The delegation are said to have retired in reasonably good order.

This was "One of Father Abraham's Best Uns," according to the *Washington (D.C.) Daily Constitutional Union* (7 September 1863), and it continued to be so. Given Grant's ultimate success, however, the original context was dropped, and the story became a hallmark of Lincolnian sagacity.

Political enemies, on the other hand, told stories of a president whose tasteless humor was every bit as unappealing as his appearance. Abraham Lincoln, the *Salem Essex Statesman* (11 June 1864) claimed, "is ugly in person and has an ungainly way of telling a smutty story at an exceedingly inappropriate time."[4] A difficult accusation to prove in print, but New York Copperhead publisher F. W. Feeks came as close as he probably could with "Hit at Antietam," in *Lincolniana, or the Humors of Uncle Abe*, a joke book got up for the 1864 election.

> Another story of Uncle Abe, too good to be lost, has leaked out. It seems he had accompanied a young lady to one of the hospitals in the capitol where the sympathizing creature, as in [*sic*] duty bound became interested in a wounded soldier. To all her inquiries as to the location of the wound, however, she could only get one reply, thus: "My good fellow where were you hit!" "At Antietam." "But where did the bullet strike you?" "At Antietam." "Yes, but where did it hit you?" "At Antietam." Becoming discouraged, she deputized Uncle Abe to prosecute the inquiry, which he did successfully. Upon his rejoining her, she was more curious than ever, when the President, taking both her hands in his said in his most impressive style, "'My dear girl, the ball that hit *him*, would not have injured *you*."

A bit risqué, perhaps, but the story does not reflect too badly on the president, nor do the others in the collection, unlike other books published by Feeks for an election year, such as *Abraham Africanus*, *The Lincoln (Negro) Catechism*, and *Trial of Abraham Lincoln*. Lincoln's predilection for joking did become a serious campaign issue that year, though, based upon the unfounded claim that while visiting the carnage following the battle of Antietam in September 1862 he had asked for a comic song.[5] In the months leading to the election, opposition newspapers churned out a scurrilous onslaught that gained momentum and embellishment at every turn: for example, that he had told jokes while visiting the Gettysburg battlefield in 1863 and that he had called for a "Negro" song at Antietam, all of it fuel for a hotly contested

"The COMMANDER IN CHIEF conciliating the Soldier's Votes on the Battle Field." Courtesy of the Library of Congress.

election. "Old Abe is going in for re-election on a most remarkable and funny record," the *Chicago Times* editor wrote sarcastically, "He wants to be re-elected joker."[6] A verse from "Soldier's Song to John Brown," sung to the tune of "Battle Hymn of the Republic," appearing in a book, the *Democratic Presidential Campaign Songster* (1864), could be more blunt:

> Show Abe Lincoln Antietam's bloody dell,
> Show Abe Lincoln where a thousand horses fell,
> Then tell Abe Lincoln and his comic song to go to h—l,
> And we'll all go marching home.

An 1864 lithograph cartoon titled "The COMMANDER-IN-CHIEF conciliating the SOLDIER'S VOTES on the Battle Field" elaborated on one version of the story with a vivid tableau. Unmoved by the slaughter around him, Lincoln tells his aide, Major Lamon, "sing us 'Picayune Butler,' or something else that's funny"; the cape he wears and the Scotch cap he holds are visual reminders of an earlier example of presidential poltroonery. (Lamon did accompany Lincoln to Antietam and was also his companion on the Baltimore train.) The real political intent of it all can be seen in the officer giving succor to a wounded soldier, who appears to be General George McClellan, commander of Union troops at Antietam in 1862, replaced by Lincoln soon thereafter, and Democratic candidate for president when the cartoon was published. Jokester Lincoln, however, had the last laugh: given a large majority of the soldiers' votes, he won a second term.

◊ ◊ ◊

The assassination of Lincoln less than a year after the election and less than a week after Lee's surrender in April 1865 created in the Union a wrenching contrast between the exultation of victory and the grief over the death of the president who had persevered through four years of war to preserve that union. Even his most relentless of enemies, Copperhead leaders and editors, Merrill Peterson says, "repented and acknowledged Lincoln's greatness"[7] (1994, 21). As for the Confederate president, early newspaper reports of his capture five weeks after Lincoln's death ridiculed his purported disguise but also charged him as a conspirator in the assassination and renewed demands that he be hanged. That clamor waned, however, as the myth of the "Belle of Richmond" took hold in the public imagination and became a festive celebration of the symbolic death of the Confederacy that played out in so many ways over the following months, a comic catharsis that paralleled the formal and protracted public grieving over the death of Lincoln. Ultimately and ironically, "it may have saved the life of Jefferson Davis by being transformed from the devil incarnate into a pathetic joke," Brayton Harris writes, "and four years of editorial demands for a public hanging no longer mattered" (1999, 315).

Chapter Two

HUMOR ON THE HOME FRONT

The effects of war on the home front North and South were vastly different. When the war began, the Union had superior industry, transportation, and communications; and as the war continued, those differences became magnified for the Confederacy, the consequence of many interrelated factors: the Union blockade, the disruption of transportation, a labor force depleted by an ever-broadening military draft, and the government's failure to deal with them all, given incompetent management, sectional differences, and the priority of supplying the military effort. Worse still, despite any advantages of fighting a defensive war, it meant that the Confederate home front was the battle front, creating profound privations on the part of non-combatants. It created as well a different kind of humor from that in the Union, humor about those privations and other adversities as a way of coping with them. No Northern editor needed to write, as did the editor of the *Chattanooga Daily Rebel* (3 March 1863), that laughter would make his readers fat in lean times. "With the prevailing scarcity of provisions—'laugh' is about the cheapest thing they can fatten on this spring," he wrote, and concluded with an afterthought that, while also comic, trenchantly reveals the deeper understanding of the problems so typical of much Confederate humor: "and we would not be surprised if they did not raise the price of that [laugh]." An anonymous poet said it all in his title and subtitle: "Better to Grin than to Growl, a song for the times."[1]

PROCLAMATION

GENERAL ORDERS, No. 38.

Whereas, General. JOHN FROST, aided by his **Irresistible Warriors,** "Boreas," "Hail," "Rain," "Snow," "Sleet" and "Dust," is about to

INVADE THE HOMES
OF
Loyal Northerners!

With a severity unparalleled in the annals of our Country, to **ENFORCE A DRAFT** that spares neither Age nor Sex, employing **Provost Marshals** that bid defiance to **LOCKS** and **BOLTS**; and Agents whose **SIREN** whispers through the shrinkage of a Door or Window cause countless miseries to the **Loyal People** aforesaid—

And Whereas, It is well known that a set of Heartless ALLIES of the said General J. Frost & Co. vegetate in this City under the assumed name of **COAL** (Monopolizers) **Dealers.** And said dealers in **Pennsylvania Diamonds,** anticipating the approach of the Invaders, intend to raise the price of the **BLACK NECESSITY** from Thirteen to Eighteen Dollars per ton before the DEATH of the OLD YEAR, to the great discomfort of the Poor.

Now, Therefore, This **PROCLAMATION** is issued for the purpose of **EMANCIPATING** the People from the **Tyranny** of both the elemental Intruders and **EXORBITANT**

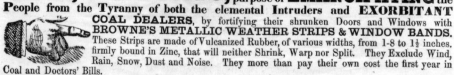

COAL DEALERS, by fortifying their shrunken Doors and Windows with **BROWNE'S METALLIC WEATHER STRIPS & WINDOW BANDS.** These Strips are made of Vulcanized Rubber, of various widths, from 1-8 to 1½ inches. firmly bound in Zinc, that will neither Shrink, Warp nor Split. They Exclude Wind, Rain, Snow, Dust and Noise. They more than pay their own cost the first year in Coal and Doctors' Bills.

They can be applied to the Tops, Bottoms, Sides and Centres of Single, Double or Sliding Doors, Windows and Sky-lights of every description. They are warranted good for 5 years, Winter and Summer.

☞ For Circular, with REFERENCE, PRICE LIST, &c., address the **Patent Weather Strip** Company's Agent,

CHARLES B. BAKER,
38 South Fifth St., Philadelphia.

WM. MANN, Printer and Stationer, 43 South Fourth St., Philada.

"Proclamation, General Orders No. 38." Courtesy of the Library Company of Philadelphia.

◊ ◊ ◊

With a few local exceptions, war did not threaten Union territory, and so a Philadelphia merchant knew potential customers would not be alarmed by the more prominent lines of his broadside advertisement. Readers would be drawn to, not alarmed by, the bold headlines and amused by puns such as "General John Frost," "draft," and "emancipating" in smaller font—all of it an inventive way to sell weather stripping for windows and doors. The conditions were real enough, but "natural," not brought on by war, although the piece gives a slight nod to wartime price gouging by coal dealers.

Confederate humor is different in that it dealt with the very real adversities of war itself. After weeks of battle, Union troops took Chattanooga in the fall of 1863, but the speaker in "The Siege of Chattanooga," in the *Charleston Mercury* (3 September 1863), makes comic light of it as a consequence of Nature. "The missiles fell about us here last week like snow flakes, and quite as harmless." He switches then to a metaphor equally harmless and dismissive: "We had shells for breakfast yesterday, and expect to take a few more on the half shell this evening, if not in batter, at least battery. I have learned to dodge these little messengers of the Yankees with astonishing agility. The other day two batteries from the other side opened on me, when I threw a double somerset as soon as I saw the smoke, and caught half a dozen conical balls in my coat tail pocket." The *Mercury* credited the story to the *Jolly Rebel*, adding that while it appeared "nowadays on something less than a quarter of a sheet" of paper, the paper was "as brimful of spirit and humor as ever." So, too, was the public face of the Confederacy itself.

The poem "Rags Ho!" in the New York *Vanity Fair* (27 December 1862) gives some idea of the difference between Union and Confederate humor on the home front. The story urges saving rags to improve the paper quality of New York newspapers that had changed "colors" because of a decline in the quality of paper, but the quips that the *Tribune* became a "sort of an Octoroon color," and the *Herald* "darker and duller" are contemporary political jibes more than concerns about rag content. The shortage of newsprint in the Confederacy, on the other hand, was real and ongoing. The quality of paper available deteriorated, page size shrank, issues were missed, and the majority of newspapers simply stopped publication. Some that survived were truly more colorful than those in New York. The files of the *Houston Tri-Weekly*

Telegraph "resemble a rainbow," Mary Massey writes in *Ersatz in the Confederacy*, printed as it was on seven different colors and shades of paper. Everyone suffered. The shortage of paper for personal letters, for example, led to the practice of "cross writing," wherein, having filled the page from left to right, the writer turned it upside down and began again. In some regions, no paper was available for marriage licenses (Massey 1993, 141, 145).

Diaries, journals, and letters recorded hardships of all kinds with personal poignancy, but the popular press responded with an uncomplaining outpouring of patriotic substitutes and recipes and making-do generally, much of it with an upbeat, humorous spirit that created a public, collective way to cope and confidence that it could. The shortage of cowhide for shoes, for example, affected civilians as well as soldiers. Although shoes were made of squirrel skin and wood with some success, dog leather was more plentiful, and dog skin shoes became something of a fad during the war, with newspapers running ads "requesting that such skins be brought to local shoemakers" (Massey 1993, 81). The problem was real, but editorial banter put a smiling public face on the straitened way of life it represented. The *Austin State Gazette* (15 October 1862) reprinted a story from the *Milledgeville (Georgia) Reporter* that "dog skins properly trimmed and tanned, make excellent shoe leather, equal to calf skin. We don't want to kill the dogs, but we want their skins, and if they can live without it, they are welcome." On its part, as the *Gazette* reported, the *Wilmington (North Carolina) Journal* had added to the jest in pointing out that "a further saving might be made if the *bark* of the dog could be used to tan his hide." (Most modern readers have no reason to know that tree bark was used to tan hides and therefore get the italicized pun.)

In response to a Virginia legislator's query if still more could be had from dead dogs, a Mr. Ferneyhough, a tanner, replied that dog oil could be extracted from the carcasses, which would be a valuable addition to niter beds badly needed by the Confederacy for producing salt peter for gunpowder. Thus "the otherwise worthless carcass of the dog can be made available in consigning to the soil of the South as a manure that far more worthless and offensive carcass, viz., the Yankee." (Reprinting the letter, the *Richmond Enquirer* [27 May 1863] added its own ironic spin, observing that it "is a Christian, gentleman-like, 'aristocratic and chivalric' view of the subject.") Except for reference to dead Yankees, it was serious business to the "practical tanner," but some Confederate newspapers took it up with tongue in check. A contributor to the *Columbus (Georgia) Enquirer* (4 October 1863) worried that Ferneyhough had not fully considered the virtues of dog oil. "The fastidious," he admitted, "may object to its use as a condiment for salads," but "why shouldn't canine be a substitute for quinine, and who shall say that . . . the active principle of dog may not turn out to be the long-sought specific for hydrophobia?" A letter to the editor of *Southern Punch* (12 October 1863) took on the hoax with an ironic tour-de-force that probed deeper into the effects of war on the Confederate home front.

To the Editor of Punch:

I read in the [Richmond] "Whig" of Tuesday the very interesting communication between a member of the House of Delegates and a carrier of this city, concerning the value of dogs. Feeling interested in this subject, and startled as I was at the estimated yield in oil and leather of 500,000 dogs, and of their immense value in dollars and cents, I am satisfied that other items of considerable importance have escaped the attention of these gentlemen, and the object of this communication is to supply the omission.

Estimating the net weight of each dog—after leather has been made of the skin and oil for the fat—to be 20 pounds, we find that 500,000 of these useful and valuable animals will yield 10,000,000 lbs. of pure lean dog; and putting this at $1.25 per lb. (which we are now paying for it in the form of Bologna sausage), we find it to amount to the extraordinary sum of $12,500,000!

I am assured that fiddle strings can be made of the entrails of these animals, fully equal to those sold in our stores, at comparatively little cost. A machine would have to be constructed, and men detailed from the army for their manufacture; but these are small matters when the profits or benefits arising there from are considered. Putting down each dog as good for twenty strings, at $1.50 each, the sum of $15,000,000 is easily realised. Were the Commonwealth to go into this business, not only would General Stuart's bango [sic]-player be supplied with strings at the cost of manufacture, but night would no longer be made "hidous [sic]"; harmony would take the place of discord and an oft repeated slander against an unfortunate race would be refuted forever. Nor must it be overlooked that the bones of these useful animals make capital handles for knives and forks, and their toe-nails glue, of a very fair quality; whilst the "hair of the dog" the world over is famous for being "good for the bite," and commands, particularly early in the morning, a ready sale.

Hoping this communication may attract the attention which it deserves, and that it may be the means of inducing persons with ample capital to engage in these important branches of manufacture, I am, Mr. Punch, very truly yours,
A Practical Man

The writer begins as a rational man who becomes increasingly *irrational* despite, or rather because of, his earnest command of "facts." His precise calculations for the money to be made in fiddle strings, for example, is preposterous in itself but is compounded when one calculates that would be enough for 2,500,00 fiddles. It recalls the profoundly ironic humor of Jonathan Swift's classic "A Modest Proposal," but where Swift hoped to call attention to a problem, starvation in Ireland, in order to solve it, "A Practical Man" has no solution and is absurdist in the modern sense. Yet, perhaps not so absurdist in a society where war had lead to butcher shops selling rats as meat.

Home folks in the North fared better; there, the word "shoddy" (as a noun) was coined to refer to both the substandard goods foisted off onto soldiers and those who did the foisting. "A Choke in Time," a poem in *Vanity Fair* (23 November 1861), may be one of the earliest appearances of the word in this sense.

We learn from a correspondent with Gen. Stone's columns that
"The boys" have nick-named the army-contractors in general "Shoddies," and when any of these personages make their appearance the cry of "Shoddy! Shoddy!" goes up from all parts of the camp!
Which suggests to Vanity Fair this pleasing little thing:

If a Shoddy
Meet a Shoddy,
A-taking of his "rye,"
And a shoddy
Chokes a Shoddy
Need anybody cry!

On the contrary, quite the reverse!

"Shoddy" had nothing to do with the scarcity of raw materials but everything to do with lining the pockets of fat cats who got army contracts. With its references to "a shoddy-cloth contractor" who once

The Dream of the Army Contractor.

Old Hucklebury, the Army Contractor, lay snoozily back in his chair,
After a sumptuous dinner, such as became a millionaire.
Wines were upon the table, gathered from sundry foreign lands,
A vulgar splendor of bottles bearing curious trade-marks and brands.

At first his dream was auriferous : he fancied himself afloat,
Hauling up gold-fish, hand over hand, into a rose-wood boat ;
And as the fishes went flippety-flop among the ebony thwarts,
Their scales in yellow dollars flew off, and he pocketed them by quarts.

But, lo ! a distressing circumstance alloyed the bliss of his dream,
His clothes were turned into army cloth, and they gaped at every seam ;
And the golden dollars fell clinkety-clank from tattered trowsers and coat,
And, where they fell, they burned round holes through the bottom of the boat.

Then, as the old Army Contractor sank, with a shriek, into the deep,
He felt the grasp of a skeleton hand that doubled him into a heap,
And he heard the croak of a skeleton voice—" Look here, old Hucklebur-ee,
You never was born to be drown-ded, so come along with me !

" I am the bones of a soldi-er, as died in the sickly camp,
Reduced by the pizenous food and the clothes that didn't keep out the damp ;
Likeways the sperrits that to us was sarved, worse liquor never I see ;
The thirst was on me—I drank it, and died—and now you must drink with me !"

And then it brandished its bony hands, that skeleton yellow and dry,
Making the vitriolic parts of a deadly cock-tail fly ;
Then came the skeleton voice, again—" Drink, 'tis the cup of Hell !"——
O ! the pallid lips and the glaring eyes, as old H. awoke with a yell !

"kept a small hand-me-down store in Chatham Street and now lives on Fifth Avenue," the broadside "The Shoddy Contractor," published in New York, might well be about someone New Yorkers would recognize. In any case, the details of his lifestyle—drinking champagne at Delmonico's, his fine "stud of horses"—are all part of the stereotype created in popular culture.

> You can tell him in a thousand by his lofty mien and tread
> This shoddy cloth contractor who has his country bled;
> But tho' justice may be sleeping, still she is not dead,
> And soon with her avenging sword fall upon the heads—
> Of all shoddy contractors, of the present time.

"The Dream of the Army Contractor" in *Vanity Fair* (17 August 1861) portrays that "justice" in picture and verse, with the typically corpulent contractor, surrounded by the symbols of his ill-gotten wealth, confronted by a dead soldier draped in burial shrouds appropriately shoddy.

The Union popular media did find humor in Confederate tribulations, but the target was more often military than civilian, portraying an enemy weakened by homegrown shortcomings, as in "The Food Question Down South" in *Harper's Weekly* (9 May 1863). In the South, wartime profiteers preyed as much on civilians as they did the military. *Southern Punch* (14 November 1863) wrote of the "hundreds of thousands who speculate in the necessaries of life, and in fine, take advantage of the wants of the poor, do everything in their power to break down the Government," and (17 October 1863) laid the blame on an old enemy, "the Yankees among us," a blade that cut a wide swath: "the Jew Yankee, the Dutch-Yankee, French, Irish." Early on in the war, editorial indignation had come up with a variety of epithets that the *Dallas Herald* (25 December 1861) conveniently catalogued— "speculators," "extortioners," "blood-suckers," "vampires," and "shylocks," which seems almost comically excessive. In time, the word "extortioners" became the word of the day, and the same paper (6 May 1863) made a weak joke about such gouging: "Among the curiosities lately added to the Museum, is a mosquito's skull, containing the souls of twenty-four extortioners and the fortunes of twelve printers—nearly half full." "Recipe to Get Rid of Extortioners," in *Southern Illustrated News* (19 September 1863), was much less good natured and took a shot at inflated Confederate currency while it was at it.

THE FOOD QUESTION DOWN SOUTH.

JEFF DAVIS. "See! see! the beautiful Boots just come to me from the dear ladies of Baltimore!"

BEAUREGARD. "Ha! Boots? Boots? When shall we eat them? Now?"

"The Food Question Down South."
Courtesy of Special Collections/
Musselman Library, Gettysburg
College.

RECIPE TO GET RID OF EXTORTIONERS —Chain them to a stake, as above; pile their ill-gotten gains around them, and any passer-by will fire the mass. This will have the happy effect, both of ridding the community of their presence, and at the same time reducing the circulating medium.

"Recipe to Get Rid of Extortioners."
From *Southern Illustrated News* (19
September 1863).

People with money could buy the necessities, even the luxuries, but the great majority had to make do, and newspapers helped with practical advice offered with a humorous sensibility. The *Houston Tri-Weekly Telegraph* (27 August 1862) summed up the problem with the light-hearted, pithy phrase "'hog, hominy and homespun' [that] constituted the actual necessities of life." *The Confederate Receipt Book* (1863) did its part in that respect, with recipes for "Apple Pie without Apples" and "Artificial Oysters" as well as homemade nostrums. The operative word in the Confederacy was "substitute," and "Confederate" became a synonym for that, as in "Confederate coffee," "Confederate tea," "Confederate dresses," and "Confederate beer." Like recipes for "Rebel Bread" and "Beauregard Cake," the alternatives were "real," but such terms gave both a patriotic and fanciful tone to the truth of grinding necessity. Finding a satisfactory substitute for one "necessity" above all others preoccupied civilians and soldiers alike. "The loss of coffee afflicts the Confederates even more than the loss of spirits," Sir Arthur James Lyon Freemantle wrote in *Three Months in the Southern States*, "and they exercise their ingenuity in devising substitutes, which are not generally very successful" (1863, 76). Southern newspapers enthusiastically and doggedly reported on substitutes—acorns, rye, peanuts, okra seeds, cornmeal and grits, Cassia Occidentalis (wild coffee), peas, parsnips, and dried sweet potatoes among them—and the special preparations many required. Contributors invariably concluded with the solemn assurance that their substitute tasted better than the real thing—and was healthier, too. (Rye was the most popular, thus the great consternation caused by a widely printed letter from a Dr. Robert in the *Augusta (Georgia) Daily Chronicle and Sentinel* [15 March 1862] warning that the high percentage of phosphoric acid can bring about "all the concomitant evils of abortion.") The most whimsical recipe for wartime coffee was proposed in the *Charleston (South Carolina) Mercury* (4 February 1863). "One of our [newspaper] exchanges publishes a new recipe for making coffee, which we recommend to the steward at our boarding house. Take coffee grains and pop corn of each an equal quantity. Roast the same together. The corn will pop out, and what remains will be unadulterated coffee."

Even civilians in cities under siege endured extraordinary privations with humor. During the nearly two-month siege of Vicksburg, people lived in caves dug into the bluffs and were reduced to eating mules, horses, dogs, as well as an exceptionally foul bread made of peas. A commissary officer named Logan had sequestered some Texas beef in preparation for the onslaught, but over time they got leaner and tougher, what with being on short rations themselves. It provoked anger and anguish, naturally enough, but a Captain J. W. A. Wright came up with a wry song about the situation, "A Life on the Vicksburg Bluffs." As the third verse put it,

> Texas steers are no longer in view, mule steaks are now done
> up brown,

While pea-bread, mule roast and mule stew are our fare in
    Vicksburg town;
And the song of your hearts shall be, while the Yanks and
    their gunboats rave,
A life in a bomb-proof for me, and a tear on "old Logan's"
    grave.

Confederates could even turn Yankee jeers about the dire straits to
their advantage. Several editors reprinted from the *Chicago Tribune* (25
July 1863) a mock "bill of fare" of the "Hotel de Vicksburg," a long list
of mule prepared in various ways, including "Mule hoof soused," "Mule
brains a la omelette," "Mule tripe fried in pea meal batter," and "Mule
tongue, cold, a la Bray." Northern newspapers reprinted the derision
of a battered enemy, but so did Southern newspapers, with a conclusion that echoes the fare-thee-well bravado in the face of adversity
that characterizes much Confederate humor. "The Tribune thinks it
is a melancholy burlesque," wrote the editor of the *Weekly Columbus
(Georgia) Enquirer* (18 August 1863); "The most melancholy thing about
it is the reflection which it must suggest to a thoughtful Yankee—if
there be such an animal—on the prospect of conquering the men who
can live and jest on such fare."

Southern Punch reprinted it too, which may have been the inspira-
tion for "Bill of Fare in a Confederate Hotel" (5 September 1863). It has
a similar look, but this bill of fare casts an unblinking, sardonic *Confederate* eye upon a society debilitated at every turn by its own deval-
ued currency, inferior provisions, bribery, and extortioners.

SHYLOCK SKINFLINT, Proprietor
Board per day, ten dollars in Confederate money, because a man
might be hung if he didn't take it.
    DINNER
SOUP.
FISH.
Ochra—diluted
Aged Baked Sturgeon
    BOILED
Cheap Beef and Cabbage\Ancient Bacon and Beans
    ENTREES—*Entre nous* not about.
French for grandeur.
Liver Sauce, aux fine herbs.

Tripe fried in Batter

Stewed Kidneys, Wine Sauce.

Fried Potatoes, aux fine herbs.

GAME—In the woods.

    VEGETABLES.

Potatoes Boiled.

Onions Boiled

Tomatoes Stewed.

Corn; Hominy

Cucumbers.

Cabbage.

Rice.

Raw Tomatoes.

Lima Beans, (In Peru.)

Squash.

Articles to be had if you bribe the waiter; provided the articles are brought in market.

    ROAST

Ribs of Beef.

Veal.

Mutton.

Young Pig.

Champagne Sauce, (Cider) Ham.

Articles to be had if you can get them.

    RELISHES—No go.

    PASTRY.

Peach Pie.

Apple Pudding.

Molasses Cake.

The latter a dish for an epicurean, formerly bought at a five cent ginger cake shop by every Lilliputian Louisiana Darkie

    COFFEE.

Unadulterated Confederate Wheat.

    Servants so obliging as never to come near unless bribed or "cussed." No gong sounded for meals, because, as there is not much to eat, Propitiator don't want to make a "fuss" about them. SELAH!

"Grafted into the Army." Courtesy of the Lester
S. Levy Collection, The Sheridan Libraries, The
Johns Hopkins University.

Beneath the humor here lies a sense of a culture, a once-civil way
of life, that has irrevocably changed. At the end of this "bill of fare"
an "epicurean" of the present day must settle for "molasses cake," the
best that a slave could aspire to in an earlier time. In this conclusion,
the piece implicitly reflects upon the old order that has changed in a
most profound way.

◊ ◊ ◊

Quoting the nineteenth-century English traveler George Augusta Sala,
Mary Elizabeth Massey writes that no conflict in history was "as much
'a woman's war' as that of 1861–1865." Sala "found the women in both
camps to be 'the bitterest, most vengeful of politicians,' 'unanimous'
in their 'exasperation and implacability'" (Massey 1966, 25). A draft
commissioner in Wisconsin experienced that firsthand, according to a
story in the *Nashville Daily Union* (22 November 1862). The conscripts
"to all appearances were willing to go; but the women had no notion
of letting them, and, to prevent the possibility of such a disaster, they
made a dead set on the official with clubs, bludgeons, sticks, stones,
&c., broke his head, smashed the draft box, and in divers other ways
put the Commissioner *hors du combat*. The victim telegraphed to Mil-
waukie [sic] for protection against the Amazons."

Women could not serve in the army (although some six hundred did so in disguise), but they lead the war effort on the home front. The patriotic mother tearfully sending her son into battle was the stuff of sentimental popular literature. Henry Clay Work took a humorous approach to the subject with his popular song "Grafted into the Army," the title a play on the words of the "lone widder," who bemoans the fate of her drafted son:

> Our Jimmy has gone for to live in a tent,
> They have grafted him into the army;
> He finally pucker'd up courage and went,
> When they grafted him into the army.
> I told them the child was too young, alas!
> At the captain's forequarters, they said he would pass—
> They'd train him up well in the infantry class—
> So they grafted him into the army.

Her feelings call for some conventional sympathy, but her fractured English and her picture on the cover of the sheet music holding "the trousies he used to wear" ("The very same buttons, the patch and the tear") are comically unconventional.

Women were also enlisted in the propaganda war in ways that reinforced the image of an enemy to be fought on all fronts. Thus, the aristocratic pretensions of the Confederate enemy seemed not just bogus but gruesome as projected in depictions of blood-thirsty Southern belles. "The Rebel Lady's Boudoir," in *Leslie's Illustrated Newspaper* (17 May 1862), is graphically brutal and satirically raw. The conventional accoutrements of civility—her clothing, the bird cage, and child—clash horrifically with the fine furniture, toys, and decorative arts fashioned from the skeletal remains of Union soldiers. Confederate women, in other words, are no less guilty than their husbands in alleged atrocities.

On its part, the Southern press portrayed Union women as embodying the rampant radicalism that characterized Northern culture generally. *Southern Punch* (2 July 1864) wrote soberly of these "miscegenating Amazons of Yankee land" who could be drafted to create a line of "breastworks" behind the infantry. To what end? "Our proverbially gallant soldiers might be induced to pause and survey the novel defenses, and the Yankees taking advantage of the delay, could make a flank movement and indulge in their favorite sport of robbing

" The outrages upon the dead will revive the recollections of the cruelties to which savage tribes subject their prisoners. They were buried, in many cases, naked, with their faces downward. They were left to decay in the open air, their bones being carried off as trophies, sometimes, as the testimony proves, to be used as personal adornments, and one witness deliberately avers that the head of one of our most gallant officers was cut off by a Secessionist, to be turned into a drinking-cup on the occasion of his marriage.

" Monstrous as this revelation may appear to be, your Committee have been informed that during the last two weeks the skull of a Union soldier has been exhibited in the office of the Sergeant-at-Arms of the House of Representatives, which had been converted to such a purpose, and which had been found on the person of one of the rebel prisoners taken in a recent conflict."—*Report of the Congressional Committee on the Conduct of the War.*

THE REBEL LADY'S BOUDOIR.

LADY (reads)—" *My dearest wife, I hope you have received all the little relics I have sent you from time to time. I am about to add something to your collection which I feel sure will please you—a baby-rattle for our little pet, made out of the ribs of a Yankee drummer-boy,*" &c., &c.

5 6 B

"The Rebel Lady's' Boudoir."
Courtesy of the American
Antiquarian Society.

henroosts and burning houses." Both North and South, women who stepped out of their properly feminine sphere were branded as Amazons, which here justifies the indelicate reference to their breasts and the most heinous of female sins, from the Southern point of view, miscegenation.

Union partisans were no more high-minded when it came to disparaging patriotic women of the Confederacy, and they did not pass up the opportunity provided by the following announcement in the *Selma (Alabama) Sentinel* (1 October 1863) by John Haralson, "Agent of Nitre and Mining Bureau": "The ladies of Selma are respectfully requested to preserve their chamber lye collected about their premises for the purposes of making Nitre. Wagons with barrels will be sent around for it by the subscriber." Like dead dogs, apparently urine could be made into potassium nitrate (nitre/niter), a critical ingredient wanting in the South for manufacturing gunpowder. The need was serious, as was Haralson's solution, but it did provide some comic relief for both sides. The *Leavenworth (Kansas) Daily Times* (21 April 1864) credited the *St. Louis Union* for a poem lampooning "the shifts resorted to by the rebel authorities to acquire the materials of war."

> John Harrolton [*sic*]
> You are a funny creature;
> You've given this "cruel war"
> A new and curious feature.
> You'll have us think while every man
> Was bound to be a fighter,
> The women (bless the pretty dears,)
> Should be put to making niter.
> John Harrolton! John Harrolton!
> Where did you get the notion
> To send your barrels round the town,
> To gather up the lotion?

This was only the first stanza, though, of a broadside poem titled "Rebel Gunpowder," reportedly written by Thomas B. Wetmore, a friend of Haralson and a resident of Selma, who wrote with broad humor about the unique contribution of Confederate women.

> We think the girls do work enough
> In making love and kissing.

But you'll now put the pretty dears
To patriotic pissing!

The contribution of his countrywomen gets deadly in stanza three:

The thing, it is so queer, you know—
Gunpowder, like the crankey—
That when a lady lifts her shift
She shoots a bloody Yankee.

Haralson's response played on the name of his friend "Wetmore," but a widow from Boston seems to have had the ultimate, and partisan, word on this feminine contribution to the war effort.

Jno Haralson! Jno Haralson!
We read in song and story
That women's [sic] in all these years,
Have sprinkled fields of glory;
But never was it told before
That how, midst scenes of slaughter,
Your Southern beauties dried their tears
And went to making water.

No wonder, Jno., your boys were brave;
Who would not be a fighter
If every time he shot his gun
He used his sweetheart's nitre?
And, vice verse what could make
A Yankee soldier sadder,
Than dodging bullets fired from
A pretty woman's bladder.

They say there was a subtle smell
That lingered in the powder;
And as the smoke grew thicker,
And the din of battle grew louder
That there was found in this compound
This serious objection;
The soldiers could not sniff it in
Without a stiff e_____. (Jackson 1954, 199–201)

Plate 1. "Yankee Volunteers Marching
into Dixie." Courtesy of the American
Antiquarian Society.

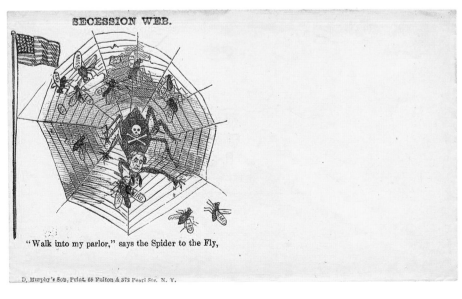

Plate 2. "Secession Web."
Courtesy of the Collection of the
New-York Historical Society.

Plate 3. Envelope of Lincoln
as a pharmacist. Courtesy of
the Collection of the New-York
Historical Society.

A SON OF MARS.

Say! Son of Mars,
With lofty figure,
Did you ever pull a trigger?
I know you didn't invent powder,
Although you talk a great deal louder.
Shun men who're really brave—
You couldn't fight your soul to save;
Go keep your tale of love untold.
For my affection's for the bold.

Plate 4. "A Son of Mars." From
the Collection of "Dreadful"
Marcia Richards.

A REGULAR.

My love is a regular man—
A man with a regular way;
He means to regulate me—if he can,
When he gets his regular pay.
But I'll be no regular's wife,
No! no! not for all creation;
For who could enjoy married life,
When bound to a mere regulation.

Plate 5. "A Regular." From the Collection of "Dreadful" Marcia Richards.

TO THE SURGEON.

Ho! ho! old saw bones, here you come,
Yes, when the rebels whack us,
You are always ready with your traps,
To mangle, saw, and hack us.

Plate 6. "To the Surgeon." From the Collection of "Dreadful" Marcia Richards.

HARD TACK.

Plate 7. "Hard Tack."
Courtesy of the American
Antiquarian Society.

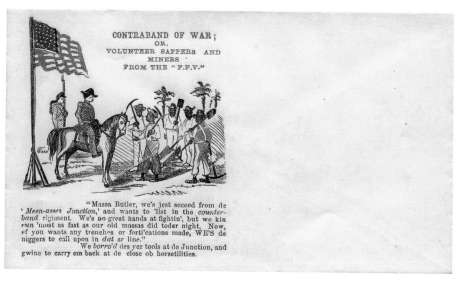

Plate 8. "Contraband of War."
Courtesy of the Collection of the
New-York Historical Society.

Men wrote virtually all of the humor during the war, but a woman's point of view made for a distinctive take on wartime conditions at home. The homemaker doing her shopping in the following story in *Southern Punch* (18 June 1864) had an appropriately salty riposte to an extortioner.

> "Mister, how do you sell your beef this morning?"
> "Why, fourteen cents a pound; how much will you have?"
> "Fourteen cents, eh? Have you got a heart?"
> "No, just sold it."
> "Well, I just knowed you couldn't have a heart an ax fourteen cents for beef."

While the most obvious humor is in the last line, the satiric heart of it is in the preceding sentence.

"Gallant Coffee," from the *Mobile Register and Advertiser* (23 April 1864), resonates with deeper irony about the far-reaching consequences of war in the South.

> Two distinguished "ossifers" of this Confederacy, while on the way from Houston to this port, lately stopped for breakfast at the residence of an old lady who has three sons in the army. Not relishing her Confederate coffee, they procured some "sure enough coffee" from their private stores. Their gallantry led them to offer a portion to the good lady of the house, accompanied with this remark: "This coffee, madam, was captured by our gallant soldiers in the Teche [Louisiana] country." The madam looked daggers at our heroes, and not only refused to accept any of the said beverage, but patriotically exclaimed: "If our gallant soldiers captured it, why don't our gallant soldiers get a chance to drink it!"

Not swayed by Cavalier condescension (a satiric dig at privileged officers who think they are above "Confederate coffee"), she takes the resolutely patriotic stand that only a mother with three sons in uniform could.

When Southern cities were occupied by Union troops, Confederate women did have their say about it in imaginative ways, serious business to them, but the consequences could be humorous. In New Orleans, for example, they treated occupying troops with verbal contempt and haughtily forced Yankee soldiers off the sidewalks with a phalanx of femininity. Commanding General Benjamin Butler nipped such behavior in the bud with his infamous "Woman's Order," declaring that such women would "be regarded and held liable to be treated as a woman of the town plying her avocation." (The nickname "Beast" quickly replaced "Spoons," so-called because of Butler's allegedly pilfering of Southern silverware.) The assault upon the virtue of Southern womanhood provoked hues and cries in the Confederate press, of course, but another story made the rounds with a laugh on Butler. At the invitation of a woman "dressed in the latest fashion and sparkling with jewelry," he called at her residence, "a fine mansion in a fashionable part of the city." Soon thereafter, the *San Antonio Semi-Weekly News* (17 July 1862) was pleased to say that he learned "he had been paying his respects to one of the most celebrated *bagnios* [brothels] in the State." In another occupied Southern city, obstreperous rebel women opened themselves up to sarcasm about as tasteless as a newspaper could get: "Some of the furious she rebels of Nashville are ugly, scrawny, lank, and toothless old girls who can't attract the notice of the Union soldiers. They are the worst of rebels, 'without an if—or a but,'" the *Wisconsin Daily Patriot* (24 April 1862) reported, quoting the *Nashville Union*.

"She rebels" *were* "the worst of rebels" because nothing *could*, really, be done about them given Union male sensibilities, "Beast" Butler to the contrary. Baltimore was not occupied in the same sense as New Orleans but did harbor a large contingent of Confederate women who also flaunted publicly their loyalties and their contempt for Federal soldiers. The song sheet "Dedicated to the She Rebels of Baltimore" (to the tune "Yankee Doodle," appropriate Union music "to teach She Rebels manners") invoked the name of General Butler, but was better spirited and cut more broadly, accusing the offenders of being spies, of having "blabbing mouths," and of chiding rebel men in the city for letting their women take the fore. The "Moral" at the end reduces the matter to the most fundamentally antifeminist terms in nineteenth-century thinking: women should stay in their "true station," their sphere:

> Now Rebel women warning take,
> By the fate of these she *hosses*,
> Let *Babies* take up all your time,
> But dont you be the *bosses*.
> For lovely women we declare,

Must move in their true station,
Their virtues when they grace their homes
Will win our admiration.

In Baltimore it became something of a literary war between the sexes. "A Volunteer Zouave" took the women of that city to task in his poem "A.D. 1862, or How They Act in Baltimore" for behavior unbecoming to their gender:

What does it mean where womanhood is taste,
The good and beautiful is left to waste?
With minds unsex'd they wildly rage of late,
And make it fashionable now, to hate.

This provoked a response, "A.D. 1862, or The Volunteer Zouave in Baltimore." Ostensibly the work of "An Officer of the 'Guards,'" it pokes fun at "this most amorous Zou-Zou," this "lady-killer" from New York who pouted poetically when Baltimore belles rebuffed him.

More serious patriotic misbehavior by Confederate belles worried a writer in *Frank Leslie's Illustrated Newspaper* (9 May 1862). "A Company of Fair Rebels" recounted the exploits of rebel spies Belle Boyd and Bell Jamieson, condemning them as feminism gone wild. Such women "signalized themselves by a reckless disregard of the holiest instincts of their sex, characteristic of the criminality of the cause they serve." In contrast, "our Northern women have shown their devotion to the cause of their country by every description of feminine heroism." Perhaps, but Dorthea Dix, appointed Superintendent of Nurses in April 1861, had to contend with skeptical male military officials who thought such duty inappropriate to women's sphere. She satisfied some by recruiting plain-looking women over thirty and invoking a dress code calling for drab, hoop-less dresses and forbidding curls and jewelry. More appealing women, though, created another concern. The popular media had long upbraided such women as preoccupied with the accoutrements of femininity—beauty and fashion—but the war provided a newly self-righteous indictment: it was unpatriotic. The poem "Rags Ho!" for example, reproached them for not donating their "rags" to making paper for newsprint:

Oh! ye teetering belles
Who wear numberless ells

Of entirely superfluous linens,
Can't you spare a few robes
From those swinging half globes.

Cartoons of cowardly swells and corpulent contractors underscored
the satire by showing them accompanied by winsome women dressed
to the nines.

The Civil War certainly did not engender anything like the "Rosie
the Riveter" image of World War II, but with so many men away at
the battle front, the door opened for women to take their places on
the home front. That kind of "feminine heroism," as the *Leslie's* article
above called it, however, created a new threat to established notions of
gender propriety that was treated with the same old raillery. A writer
in *Frank Leslie's Illustrated Newspaper* (27 September 1862) worried
that women "of late are expected to be both men and women at once,"
including doctors, architects, apothecaries, as well as cooks, carpen-
ters, and more. "The truth is, woman has her own sphere, which, in this
country at least, she fills rather gracefully and agreeably (albeit with
a redundancy of crinoline), and is generally, as she ought to be, con-
tented with her lot." "Cato," in the *Geneva (New York) Gazette* (4 March
1864), worried about what he called the coming "Gyn kokracy," a dis-
ease that "manifests itself in absurd endeavors of women to usurp the
places and execute the functions of the male sex." At heart, "Cato" may
have been serious, but his comic exaggeration—"Gynœkokracy"?—
has a humorous, if satiric, tone.

In the North, the war created an oddly conflicted response to
women and their proper place: pretty women were feminine but unpatriotic; homely women were feminists but patriotic. The title of W.
O. Eaton's "A Female War Club—A Significant Sign of the Times," in
Yankee Notions (May 1862), speaks directly and satirically to the newly
worrisome state of affairs. Most of the women of the "Punktown
Female War Club" see the war as furthering their personal cause. For
Mrs. Bantam it is an act of Providence, one meant "to make men sub-
jick to women, who are fast becoming the great majority in the world,
owing to wars which are killing off men." And "when the wars are all
over," she concludes, "there will be so few men left that women will
get their rights, and then we shall rule as we ought to." When they
start an enthusiastic discussion on the "proper costume" for ladies in
uniform, "ideas began to look practical, original, and womanly," Eaton
writes. Bantam, however, gets them back to the real agenda: "that we

What shall be done with the **Young Men who won't go if Wanted** ?
We'll shave their heads and keep 'em at home, and make 'em scrape lint for heroes— under charge of a competent female. [Competent female in back ground.]

PATER FAMILIAS.—"*Home Guards indeed ! We don't need them. I and the girls will attend to that.*"

"What Shall be done with the Young Men who won't go if wanted?" Courtesy of the Library Company of Philadelphia.

are a superior being, and that war is designated to give us our rights at last. Think what a sublime spettikle we present here in the nineteenth centoory, and going on to the twentieth, a band of women riz up here to defend our country, and teach the men-folks to do their duty. . . . I have no doubt that there isn't a woman here but might yet be President of the United States, if we keep the ball rolling." Truly radical stuff for the time, and typically the women who are most radical are the least feminine in the conventional sense. One is "a broad-backed, coarse-featured woman, with an arm like a leg of mutton"; the outspoken Bantam is a "sharp-eyed, sharp-voiced woman—who never agreed with her husband upon anything since they were married, and whose tones affected her hearers like a shower-bath of vinegar." Of course, her laughable way of speaking undermines any possible credibility to what she says. Eaton tells his story with broad, dismissive lines of caricature, but as the title says, that story is "A Significant Sign of the Times."

"The War," in the *Comic Monthly* (June 1861), lampoons men who shirk their military duty by condemning them to women's work, the usual take on that matter, but it illustrates a more alarming consequence: when men will be women, women will be men. The fellow in the left panel has the iconic mutton chops of the stereotypical cowardly swell, here appropriately relegated to women's work and therefore "under charge of a competent female," which seems to mean that she looks male. In the right panel we see "pretty" women as home guards, but the pugnacious, homely, sword-wielding woman who does not "need" men, as she says, dominates the scene. The war did unsettle gender roles in the North, and the title of the piece has more do with that than with the war on the Confederacy.

Henry Clay Work's sheet music "We'll Go Down Ourselves" (1862), on the other hand, raises no alarms about militant women, perhaps because it addresses a specific issue, the failure of the Union army in 1862 to cross the Potomac and take Richmond. (Perhaps, too, because Work was an abolitionist who was also not threatened by activist women.) Neither coquettes nor single-minded feminists, these women have no agenda but to end the war.

> "What shall we do, as years go by,
> And Peace remains a stranger—
> With Richmond yet in rebel hands,
> And Washington in danger?
> What shall we do for leaders, when
> Old Age this race is cropping?"
> I asked whom I met—
> And didn't it set them hopping!
>
> Chorus: "What shall we do? What shall we do?
> Why, lay them on the shelves,
> And we'll go down ourselves,
> And teach the rebels something new,
> And teach the rebels something new."
>
> "What shall we do when all the men
> For battle have enlisted—

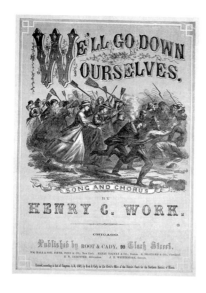

"We'll Go Down Ourselves." Courtesy of
the Lester S. Levy Collection, The Sheridan
Libraries, The Johns Hopkins University.

And yet the rebels hold their ground,
And law is yet resisted?"

Instead of doing as I should—
The theme politely dropping,
I ventured yet one question more—
Oh didn't it get them hopping!

The confrontation of male authority is forthright and certainly sassy—
it gets "them hopping"—but only on the matter at hand. (The "one
question more" is tantalizingly ambiguous, however.) And while we
laugh at the men on the cover of the sheet music, they *are* the Confederate enemy, after all, their bayonets no match for Federalist females
wielding brooms, appropriately representative of their proper sphere.

◊ ◊ ◊

Men wrote virtually all of the humor of the war and drew the cartoons,
but women did have an authentic and humorous "angle of vision" on
the war in two very different ways: the *Waterford News* and comic valentines. Eight issues of the *News* appeared intermittently in the last
months of the war, the work of three young Quaker women in Waterford, Virginia, on the northern boundary of that Confederate state.[2] An

"underground" paper sympathetic to the Union and printed in Balti-more, the *Waterford News* had the personal stamp of its editors in every respect. Spirited editorials chided the bumptious behavior of the "chiv-alry" and "rebels" in the town, but there is also a low-key, less conten-tious humor appropriate to the youth and Quaker convictions of the editors. A column titled "Marriages" reads, "Young men, will you see this 'should be interesting' place vacant, when you could so easily rem-edy it?" followed by several inches of blank space, a running jest that took a variety of forms. The series reflects the half-serious interests of the unmarried editors but also the serious fact that young Quaker men had left the area rather than be conscripted into the Confederate army. Another running story concerned a mud hole in the heart of town, implicitly the work of thoughtless rebels. "Being fearful the gentlemen will get their feet muddy, the ladies will try to remedy it," the editors promised. A letter from a local pig, however, offered a different point of view: "Hitherto one of the greatest enjoyments of myself and fellow grunters, was an afternoon siesta in the mud hole on Second street, which enjoyment you have been the means of lessening by having one load of sand deposited in the deepest and most comfortable corner."

In "Shopping Under Difficulties" a woman correspondent gives a lively, humorous account of a serious problem for the community: Union loyalists needed passes to cross the Potomac to Maryland, where they could buy only ten dollars worth of things not available in the Confederacy. She takes on the responsibility—"instead of my hus-band," she says, "because I knew he would spend all of the ten dollars on some foolishness and tobacco." Practical and direct, she speaks with an honestly feminine voice of a real woman's experience. "I got in the wagon, and lending a deaf ear to his [husband's] repeated injunctions to 'not let the horse run away with you,' I flourished my hickory and with a 'gee-up' we started." Her detailed catalog of purchases no doubt accurately represents what a family in such circumstances would need, as well as want, but the author also spins entertaining fiction from the experience. Her husband was "really suffering for shirts," but she bought him a half plug of tobacco to keep him quiet about them, which figures into the conclusion describing her return: "It would have done your hearts good to see the children over their candy and cakes, whilst husband's smile deepened into a broad grin when I handed him the tobacco, and hasn't said a word about shirts yet." Through it all, she negotiates the domestic consequences of war with good humor and feels empowered by doing so.

It was the editors' unbending support of the Union cause, though, that probably provoked critics (implicitly Confederate) to accuse them of that catch-all sin, "women's rights." Although only eight intermittent issues of four pages were published, the *Waterford News* had a hearing far beyond a small Virginia town. Proceeds of sales were donated to the U.S. Sanitary Commission, which provided care for wounded Union soldiers. *New York Tribune* editor Horace Greeley sang the praises of the young, patriotic "girls" in occupied territory, and President Lincoln reportedly saw a copy (Chamberlin et al. 1999, iii).

Comic valentines, curiously enough, gave women a forum to have their say about the war. Before the war, comic valentines, sent anonymously and offensive to defenders of public taste and decorum, became nearly as popular as the "sentimentals," as traditional valentines were called. "These caricatures were a kind of extortion," Leigh Eric Schmidt writes, "especially when directed at women: Behave modestly and decorously or suffer the consequences of social rejection, ridicule, or even violence," a popular phenomenon "coincident with the first wave of organized struggle for women's rights in the late 1840s and 1850s" (1995, 84, 85). War, though, was a masculine enterprise and created a market for valentines for women to voice a wide range of opinions about the men who received them. Some spoke to a soldier worthy of the affection of the saint's day, a light-hearted compliment to sentimental valentines with much the same point, and were probably signed. Other valentines, more likely sent anonymously, given the message in picture and words, supported the war effort with a feminine conviction: no faint-of-heart man could win the heart of a patriotic woman (see plate 4). No self-important, military posturing with the soldier pictured in "A Regular" (see plate 5), but the verse, with its witty play on the military term "regular," has more feminist import in its forthright rejection of conventional notions of marriage.

◊ ◊ ◊

Humor on the home front North and South differed because conditions were so very different. From the beginning of the war and over the next four years, privations dominated every aspect of the daily life of everyone in the Confederacy, and while humor could not have made that life any easier, it was a way to acknowledge that reality without surrendering to it. The Union and the Confederacy celebrated Christmas differently in 1862. Mary McCrimmon's poem "Santa Clause," in

"Santa Clause in Camp."
Courtesy of Special
Collections, University of
Virginia Library.

the *Southern Illustrated News* (27 December 1862), begins with a fond recollection of Christmases past and Santa's visit to children in the South with a cornucopia of toys and candy: "all received something—and no one a switch." Not this Christmas, though, thanks to the mischief of mean-spirited Yankees:

> Our ports are blockaded, and Santa, to-night,
> Will hardly get down here; for if he should start,
> The Yankees would get him unless he was *smart*:
> They beat all the men in creation to *run*,
> And if they could get him, they'd think it fine fun
> To put him in prison, and steal the nice toys
> He started to bring to our girls and our boys.

The blockade would have made Christmas lean in the Confederacy, certainly, but "A Bright Christmas Thought from One of Our Little Friends," in the *San Antonio Herald* (27 December 1862), while less fanciful than McCrimmon's poem, is more typical of Confederate humor in its frank acknowledgement of the effect of war on life at home. As this story goes, "A little six-year-old, in speaking of Christmas the other day remarked that he did not expect to get any thing this time, as he reckoned *Old Santa Claus was a Conscript* and had been sent to the wars."

For the Union that year, on the other hand, Santa's bag was brim full, at least according to Thomas Nast's cover for *Harper's Weekly* (3 January 1863) titled "Santa Claus in Camp." No lack of presents for these "boys," and with St. Nick's entertaining them with a caricature of Jefferson Davis as a marionette, the string around his neck a traitor's noose, we know which side Santa is on.

Chapter Three

CIVIL WAR, WAR HUMOR

"War is at best barbarism. Its glory is all moonshine," retired Union General William Tecumseh Sherman told the graduating class at the Michigan Military Academy in 1879, and he concluded with what has become the most famous judgment of armed conflict: "War is hell." So very succinct, and a truth invoked since by both those who oppose war and those who, however reluctantly, accept its necessity. Even if we have not been in battle, we "know" it is true in the same way we know that humor is a way of coping with something so horrific. In doing so in the Civil War, humor is often free of partisan passions because it deals with the many and various vicissitudes of being a soldier no matter what cause he fought for. Becoming a soldier (or avoiding it), being in battle and getting killed or wounded, the rigors of soldiering, the numbing boredom of camp life—all of them new, unsettling realities that soldiers of each side had to deal with. And although this was humor about the soldiers and, in part, for them, it was most often written by and for those at home. The quip "United we sleep, divided we freeze" appeared in newspapers on both sides, expressing with some wit a real hardship on the part of the soldiers but also an implicitly patriotic solidarity for survival that would comfort folks at home.

Humor on one subject, though, was written solely by and for soldiers, humor about imprisonment. For prisoners of war, humor was crucial to creating some semblance of normalcy under conditions so abnormal. Confederates incarcerated at Fort Delaware produced in

April 1865 one copy of a handwritten, three-column newspaper titled the *Prison Times* (The war ended the next month). Union prisoners at Libby Prison in Richmond formed the "'Richmond Prison Association' to supervise their life, to make rules for cleanliness, and to furnish entertainment." The official seal represented the sardonic truth: a circle of lice with the Latin motto translated as "Bite and Be Damned" (Hesseltine 1930, 60). At Camp Ford in Tyler, Texas, Union prisoners put out a handwritten newspaper, *Old Flag* (1864), with the hope of "enlivening the monotonous, and at times unbearably eventless life of Camp Ford."[1] With many of the "departments" of a conventional newspaper—"local" news, jokes about prison life, and mock commercial notices among them—*Old Flag* created some semblance of home. Given that only one hand-written copy of each issue was issued and read aloud "at the various cabins," it made the editor's repeated, indignant remonstrance against unpaid subscribers a running joke and a parody of hometown newspapers of the time, here an "inside joke," as it were. Prison humor was, in fact, arcane, with references to people, events, and conditions that only men living in such singular circumstances could know and therefore "get." A prisoner at Libby Prison composed a long "Prison Bill of Fare," the formal poetic structure and diction an ironic contrast to the mock appreciation of the barely edible provender to be had in prison. Most of what the 160 lines are about puzzles modern readers (and amateur poetry does not help), but the description of the rations of bread and meat is clear enough:

> Our friends sends us loaves that are unique and neat,
> Our loving eyes upon the "batch" we fix,
> And quietly eat our rations—ounces six.

Meat rations are equally meager:

> Three ounces of some butchered cow:
> How late, deponent saith not—but the smell
> Would indicate it hard to tell.[2]

◊ ◊ ◊

Death, the ultimate hell of war, haunted soldiers and those who loved them, and it dominated sentimental popular culture, an industry in its own right. Humor came as close as it could to dealing with the real thing, and *how* close had much to do with how "humorous." Authenticating details helped do that, as in the following from *Harper's Monthly* (March 1862):

> "We had been encamped in Indianapolis," writes one of the brave boys, "about a month before we left for the seat of war. Some time after we arrived in Virginia we heard that quite a large number of letters for the regiment were detained at Indianapolis for the postage. While passing through the camp one day, I overheard a couple of soldiers conversing about those letters. One inquired, 'what would be done with them?' The other replied, 'I suppose they will be sent to the dead-letter office, and after we get killed we can get them.' Thanks to the bad aim of the rebels, only three of as brave a regiment as ever went to the field had to call at *that* office for their mail matter."

Playing on "dead-letter," the anecdote acknowledges the reality of death but defies it with humor, for soldiers and loved ones alike— anyone, really, who read the story in the most popular magazine of the day.

A humorous, tour-de-force treatment of death and war is "Extracts from a Soldier's Letter, Camp Winder, Richmond, Va., Sunday night, Nov. 1 1863," by "Marengo" to "Crip" in *Southern Punch* (14 November 1863). Like the letter format itself, the details—the location (a hospital in Richmond), a specific date, even the time of day—give initial credibility to what becomes increasingly *in*credible. Not merely clever, this is artfully crafted literary irony at its best that needs to be read in full.

> You remember the last time I saw you, I told you that if Heaven spared me, I'd write to you, provided I ever stopped long enough in one place. Well, that time has at length "arrove," and with a heart teeming with kind memories and genial sentiments, I "perceed" to the performance of the proposition propounded. First of all then, you will desire to know if I am still alive, and some little of my history since we parted. I have been killed several times, but made out to remain with my regiment "purty tolerable spunctual," until the big old He fights around Richmond, when I was effectually and essentially slaughtered.
>
> Since that time, I have been off and on, dead and partly alive alternately. I know you have suffered a great deal, and I allude to

your infirmities with feelings of delicate regard. You doubtless think that "rheumatiz" is about as tight a little paper as death can be put up in. "Lord bless your soul, chile," it is no more to compare a regular attack of Bung shells than an ordinary Belly ache, in green apple time, is to an old fashioned out and out tooth pulling. Now, a man with rheumatiz, knows just exactly what he's got and what to depend upon, and then he most usually has time to grunt, be sorry, complain of his fate, and tell his friends good bye. Not so with Bung shells, because you see, it ain't them that hits him, and kills him, but nine times out of ten, he dies of pure suspicion and sadness. Minnie balls and grape shot and cannister, are a real relief under them circumstances, even if they do kill a feller in three or four places, because you see the noise they make is just as much better suited to the taste of civilized humanity, as the whistle of a nightingale is more pleasant than the bass notes in the growl of a brindle Bengal tiger.

Crip, I wish I could just see you long enough to tell you about how I died, and how scared I was. After that Bung shell hit me, your old hat full of grape and minnies wouldn't have made me stir the eighth of an inch from behind the cornstalks where I fell. I reckon you would not suppose that a single cornstalk was much protection. Don't fool yourself, sir, corn is right high now, in these parts, and meal in Richmond is twenty dollars a bushel; but under those circumstances, stalks would out sell 'em all holler. Reality ain't nothing to war. If it was, war would lose more than half its glory. It's the noise that kills fellers principally, and it's the most awful death a man can die. Therefore, he deserves all the credit which a generous and grateful country can render to his remains.

Well, as I was going to tell you, after I was killed the last time, the doctors all said I was killed entirely, too much even to be fit for anything else: so they sent my remains to Alabama on furlough, where they were kept by the ladies until just before the last fight at Fredericksburg, when you know, the Big General wrote to Mr. Shorter and the ladies, to send up all the dead, wounded and missing, as well as the live fellers, as he had a use for all sorts.

My remains were sent up with the balance, and arrove just in time for the fight; but seeing as how I was already badly killed, they did not shoot me any more jest then, but skared me all over rite good agin; and when the fellers all went up with Mister Mead to the North, my remains were sent back and handed around, until

Mister Dix and his drapshot gang commenced stealing the poultry and tear up holler bridges around Richmond again.

I couldn't stand this; so I volunteered, with a whole lot of crippled fellers, to come over here, just resolved to eat them up "bodaciously"—but the porky scoundrel found out that we had got here, and left. So my corpus was brought back to Richmond, and here I am.

Faithfully yours,

Marengo

The piece is Confederate not only in many factual details, but also in reflecting the feeling of many in the Confederacy late in 1863 that continued carnage was futile. At the same time, though, it speaks to any battle-weary soldier's sense of being "used," as Marengo says, in so many mindless ways, according to the whims of others—despite, as Marengo also says, his being so emphatically "dead"! The matter-of-fact, sometimes folksy way of speaking about being mortally wounded again and again creates a fatalistic, even absurdist point of view about death and this war and is stark testimony to the truth of Sherman's famous dictum about war in general.

◊ ◊ ◊

Second only to the fear of dying was the fear of being wounded. "Rare comedy was intermingled with the tragedy of battle," William Bickham wrote in *Rosencrans' Campaign with the 14th Army Corps* (1863); "The humorism of battle saturates you after carnage is ended, and when the dead are buried. The richest of fun is not printable. But soldiers roar over awkward adventures of their comrades when they assemble in their bivouacs." Although not "rich," the following was "printable."

A group of mangled soldiers were sauntering around a field hospital waiting for temporary bandages to be applied to their wounds. The surgeon was fully occupied, and some delay was unavoidable. A brawny trooper, with a bullet in his left leg and a ball in his right arm, hobbled up to the surgeon, holding his wounded arm with his left hand. Projecting his mutilated leg he said, with laughable grimace, "Well, doctor, the d——d rebs come pretty near hittin' me." Another fellow, who had lost the end of his nose, elbowed his way into the circle, spouting blood as a whale spouts water, and

convulsed the group: "The d——d rascals"—sputter—"doctor"—
sputter—"came d——d near"—sputter—"*missin'* me." (Bickham
1863, 359, 360)

Getting wounded horrified Civil War soldiers because the primary
ammunition in play, the Minié bullet, was meant to maim and inca-
pacitate as much as to kill. Also, given the state of medicine in general
and under battlefield conditions in particular, amputation was the
most expedient way of dealing with most injuries. The photographic
images of stacks of limbs outside of hospital tents haunt us today, as
they did soldiers and their families during the war. Virtually all comic
valentines are, well, essentially "comic," but both the illustration and
the verse in "To the Surgeon" (see plate 6) speak all too vividly to the
horrors of being wounded. The grinning skull dominates, but the tools
of his trade are clearly delineated, giving visual meaning to the word
"sawbones."

Amputation itself would be too gruesome to portray visually and
humorously. A picture, for example, would overwhelm the witty word
play, beginning with the title, in the following poem in *Harper's Weekly*
(26 September 1863), reportedly written by a soldier who had lost a leg
at the Battle of Fair Oaks.

> "L-E-G on My Leg"
> Good leg, thou wast a faithful friend,
> And truly hast thy duty done;
> I thank thee most that, to the end
> Thou didst not let this body run.
> Strange paradox, that in the fight
> Where I of thee was thus bereft,
> I lost my left leg for the Right,
> And yet the right's the one that's left!
> But while the sturdy stump remains,
> I may be able yet to patch it,
> For even now I've taken pains
> To make an L-E-G to match it.

Soldiers in the field were not loath to have a laugh at the expense of
medical authority. Wrapping up a story titled "The Yells of Our Army,"
the *Charleston Mercury* (9 November 1863) reported, "Whenever a surgeon approaches a regiment, a by-stander would think that the annual

migration of all the ducks in the universe had commenced, and that they were concentrated in that particular spot, for the air resounds with 'quack, quack, quack,' and the unfortunate quack, I beg his pardon, I mean surgeon, rides off, endeavoring to preserve his dignity as best he can." An anecdote in the *Keene (New Hampshire) Sentinel* (11 June 1863) that got passed around in the papers also showed little respect for medical skills.

> An amusing thing occurred in the Twenty-fourth Ohio. A few days since, a soldier in passing to the lower part of the encampment, saw two others from his company making a rude coffin. He inquired who it was for.
>
> "John Bunce," said the others.
>
> "Why," replied he, "John is not dead yet. It is too bad to make a man's coffin when you don't know if he is going to die or not."
>
> "Don't trouble yourself," replied the others. "Dr. Coe told us to make his coffin, and I guess he knows what he give him."

Even though no John Bunce seems to have served in the Twenty-fourth Ohio, the story would ring true for soldiers on either side.

◊ ◊ ◊

In the patriotic heat following the fall of Fort Sumter in 1861 most people, North and South, believed that the war would be brief, and volunteers clamored to join up. By the next year, however, both the Union and the Confederacy had to call for a draft of the "able-bodied," a term that became increasingly inclusive over the years, more critically in the South given the unrelenting attrition of limited manpower. For both armies, avoiding the draft was serious business and that meant comic ridicule of those who tried. "How Conscription Operates in East Tennessee," a story in the *Nashville Union* (14 November 1862), found it "amusing to hear the enrolling officers tell how the conscripts talk and act, when they [enrolling officers] call on them for their names, age, etc. . . . There are more hip-shot, string-halted, broken-legged, knock-kneed, and rheumatic-stricken young men through our country than were ever known to infest any country before." Sounds like the real thing, but some anecdotes are jokes about draft dodgers and their outrageously inventive ways of avoiding soldiering. The *Savannah (Georgia) Republican* (16 October 1862) reprinted from the *Zanesville (Ohio)*

Simpkins practis in njsanity before a g'ass.   Consternation of his domestic.

Drummer, in order to escape the conscription, dons female attire and keeps a candy-store.

Young Wapshot—his appearance before and after the passing of the Conscription Act. Rapid approach of old age.

A MANUFACTURED ACCIDENT.

ALARMED WIFE—"*Dear, dear! George, what's the matter? What has happened to your leg and arm?*"
HUSBAND (*in a whisper*)—"*Hush, Minnie!—it's all right. I've only put these things on to bother the conscription man; he's 'ust behind.*"

IN DREAD OF THE LAW.
BOY (to Druggist)—"*Have you anything good for turning the hair grey?*"

May. 1863.

O'Rafferty, to avoid the rigor of Conscript Law, enlists in a travelling troupe, and enacts the role of a performing elephant. The above cartoon exhibits him at the moment when he is making himself known to an old friend.

"The Conscription in Prospect—
The Would-Be Exempt." Courtesy
of the Library Company of
Philadelphia.

The way Mr. Slowly procured an Exemption from Conscription.

Mr. Slowly determines to evade conscription, and drinks three gallons of Lager Beer per day, for the accomplishment of his plan. As he appeared one month before the Conscript Law went in force.

Fearing the result of an examination, he increases the allowance to four gallons per day. His appearance two weeks after increasing the dose. Lager Beer is now the only nourishment he partakes of.

Mr. Slowly is taken before the Conscript board, examined by the physicians, and exempted. Medical Certificate certifies that "Mr. S. has premonitory symptoms of dropsy."

"The Way Mr. Slowly Procured an Exemption from Conscription." From *Southern Punch* (14 November 1863).

Courier the story "An Exempt," one whose plea "was picked up near the desk of the Drafting Commissioner's office in that city: I certify that I am lame, have a broken back, hip out of joint, a cracked arm, and am railroad engineer, am clerking in the Post Office; also have charge of a telegraph office, and a wife and baby, and am opposed to fighting—have joined the Quakers." The more lame the excuse, the more satirical. "Among the excuses for exemptions," the *Atlanta Intelligencer* reported, "some are extremely ludicrous. In Smyth County, Virginia, we learn, one man, in enrolling himself, wrote opposite his name, 'one leg too short.' The next man that came in, noticing the excuse, and deeming it pretty good, thought he would make his better, and wrote opposite his name, 'Both legs too short!'" (quoted in Moore 1862, 13). In the North, the *Madison (Wisconsin) Daily Patriot* (24 April 1862) version of the story tacked on a joke on the enemy by concluding that the fellow "had been reading some of the exploits of the southern armies, doubtless, and supposed legs to be the first essential."

Avoiding the draft, in other words, sometimes made for humor that often had little to do with its serious implications. "The Conscription in Prospect—The Would-be Exempt" in *Leslie's Budget of Fun* (May 1863) filled a page of six comic illustrations portraying how some men tried to weasel their way out of serving their country: faking injury, madness, age, and the like, some of them legitimate reasons, actually,

THE NEW "SOCIAL EVIL."

Small Swell.—" Dweadful boaw, this Dwaft. Dwags a fellah fwom the boozum of his Club !"

"The New 'Social Evil.'" Courtesy
of Special Collections/Musselman
Library, Gettysburg College.

"Costume Suggested for the Brave Stay-at-Home-Light-Guard." Courtesy of Special Collections, University of Virginia Library.

but treated contemptuously here. Inventive skulkers in the Confederacy came in for their share of graphic contempt, as in "The Way Mr. Slowly Procured an Exemption from Conscription" in *Southern Punch* (14 November 1863).

The most disgraceful accusation that could be leveled against cowards was that such men were not "men" at all. In "The New 'Social Evil,'" in *Vanity Fair* (6 September 1862), the "Small Swell" complains, "Dweadful Boaw, this Dwaft. Dwags a fellah fwom the boozum of his club." The tall, masculine fellow in military dress wordlessly dominates the shorter "swell," whose mannered way of speaking identified him as the effete, effeminate male stigmatized in nineteenth-century popular culture.

Members of the "home guard" or militia were treated with similar contempt. Oliver Wendell Holmes gave the title "The Sweet Little Man" to a poem on these "Stay-At-Home-Rangers":

A SAD STATE OF AFFAIRS.

NUMBER ONE.—The military have all the aces and won the trick this time! I bought a substitute, and here I am in limbo, for State service.

NUMBER TWO.—No more nice lunches for me. Army fare for the rest of the war, I suppose.

NUMBER THREE.—And no more Old Rye! What was I thinking about that I didn't get a commission as quartermaster a year ago. I might have had a big farm and lived like a lord!

NUMBER FOUR.—Deuce take it, Spades is the band hereafter. I suppose some General will keep a fellow digging along until Old Abe cries quit.

NUMBER FIVE.—Exactly so. A fellow won't be allowed to take a drink of even strichnine in the army, unless he steals it.

NUMBER SIX.—A pretty game of poker it will be, having a Yankee bayonet playing poker under a man's diaphram.

NUMBER SEVEN.—We all have substitutes in the army, and here the Judges are deciding that a man must leave his comfortable quarters and go into the "milish" and do duty like a regular soldier!

"A Sad State of Affairs." Courtesy of The Library of Virginia.

> Bring him the buttonless garment of woman!
> Cover his face lest it freckle and tan;
> Muster the apron-string Guards on the Common,
> That is the corps for the sweet little man!

Men who dodged combat were a natural for visual satire. The cartoon "Costume Suggested for the Brave STAY-AT-HOME LIGHT GUARD," in *Harper's Weekly* (7 September 1861), was one of many. The cook pot in place of the military hat, brushes as epaulets, the conventional sword as a duster, a broom where a rifle should be, all of it representing a willfully emasculated male, emphasized by the pinched waist and billowing dress. Only the facial hair suggests that this is a man, albeit a swell.

North and South, draft dodgers of any yellow stripe were held up to ridicule, but in the Confederacy shirking military duty made worse the very real problem of a dwindling number of available men. Those in "A Sad State of Affairs," in *Southern Punch* (5 September 1863), are less comically portrayed than the "light guard," what with their lame, self-serving objections to the government's broadening yet again eligibility for military duty. The drawing has the usual artistic limitations of Confederate engraving, but here the crudely rendered figures look as craven as what they have to say.

◊ ◊ ◊

Both sides needed draftees, but men forced to serve often did not make for good soldiers. "There was a pervasive feeling among volunteers that conscripts were second-rate soldiers," Bell I. Wiley writes; and while many proved to be first-rate, "the great majority of testimony, both of officers and privates, bristled with such uncomplimentary epithets as cowards, skulkers, shammers, useless and worthless" (1943, 342). They were obvious targets, in other words, for caustic humor. The speaker in the ironically titled Confederate song "The Valiant Conscript," performed on an Augusta, Georgia, stage in spring 1864, according to the *Augusta Daily Constitutional* (15 August 1864), has vainglorious dreams of heroic grandeur, but real battle is an abrupt awakening.

> How are you, boys, I'm just from camp,
> And feel as brave as Caesar;
> The sound of bugle, drum, and fife,

Has raised my Ebenezer.
I'm full of fight—odds, shot and shell!
I'll leap into the saddle,
And when the Yankees see me come,
Lord, how they will skedaddle.

When a rifle accidentally fires, though, he is the one who runs:

What's that? Oh dear! A boiler's burst,
A gas pipe has exploded!
May be the Yankees are hard by,
With muskets ready loaded.
On, gallant soldiers, beat them back!
I'll join you in the frolic,
But I've a chill from head to foot,
And symptoms of the cholic!

Coined in the Civil War (by Yankees), to "skedaddle" took on two different comic meanings for both sides. As in the above, it described what you planned to make the enemy do—not merely to retreat but to do so in disarray—but it was also a humorous euphemism that could take the sting out if the enemy did it to you, a comic, face-saving admission of good sense in the face of battle. The Union "Skedaddling Song" does that with a good parody of one of George Root's several sentimental songs popular on both sides, "Just before the Battle, Mother." To a tune that may still be familiar, the original begins:

Just before the battle, Mother,
I am thinking most of you,
While upon the field we're watching,
With the enemy in view.

The parody is good because it begins with what would have been the well-known, heart-tugging expectations of the first line—and then abruptly, and therefore humorously, changes the original tone. The lugubrious tune heightens the comic reversal of the lyrics.

Just before the battle, Mother,
I was drinking mountain dew;
But when I saw the Rebels marching,
Unto the rear I quickly flew.

Where all the stragglers were flying,
Thinking of their homes or wives.
It was not the Rebs they feared, dear Mother,
But their own dear precious lives.

His retreat, he assures his mother in the chorus, will be a comfort to her:

Then, farewell! Mother, you will never
See my name among the slain;
For, if I only can skedaddle,
Dear Mother, I'll come home again.

A clever parody of the sentiments of the original, it also speaks to a common-sensical desire for survival and to seeing one's mother again as it does to a cowardly retreat.[3]

This was in 1865, when heroic notions of battle and the patriotic expectations they furthered had taken a more realistic turn. In one of his several letters, "The Poit Lawriett" reported in *Southern Punch* (9 January 1864) the exploits of the "White Ploom Falanx." They attacked Bangor, "a U.S. stronghold in Maine," according to the writer, promising to "burn and slawter all the inhabitants and houses in the town, not xceptin the wimmen and littel children." The "Poit" longs for a Homer to write about what happens next, but his own style suits the mock heroic actions of the "Falanx" just fine.

The fite was desperit and bluddy until our hole army xecewted anuther stragetick move, whitch was as follers: We all turned round and went off as if we was retreetin, and to maik it look more so, we left a good menny cannons, prisoners and uther plunder, includin quarter-master stores. The pious frawd was bewtiful, for the dastardly fo began a chasin us as if they thawt we was whipped shore enuff! The Falanx flew to their favorite poast—to frunt—and conduckted what the Yanks thawt was a retreat, in a masterly stile. Sometimes we was miles ahed of evry body; nuthin could stop us, caws onner and dooty was a leading us on to glory.

The semi-literate style, inspired by the popularity of Artemus Ward in the North as well as the South, is as mockingly heroic as the "battle" it describes.

In the North, George Arnold, writing as "McArone," had contributed a long series of letters about the war to *Vanity Fair* until it folded in mid-1863, whereupon he continued them in the *New York Leader*. The pen name played upon "macaroni," a fop, and the tone of the early letters was appropriately flippant, having more to do with the dilettante persona than the war. With a letter reprinted in the *New Orleans Daily Picayune* (27 March, 1864), though, he writes his report on the siege of Richmond with the jaded pen of the writer behind the persona.

> Gen. Custer made a grand divertissement on Sunday to draw the rebel cavalry troops from us. He drew them. He got tangled on the question of roads. There used to be a very good road from the Rapidan to Spotsylvania Court House, but the rebels moved it back into the country. Custer, therefore, could not find it, and had to take to the woods all night, drawing the rebel cavalry after him. At one time they caught up with him. A desperate hand-to-hand fight began, and lasted four hours. The rebels, as is their custom, outnumbered our men five to one. Three men were partly killed, and one gently wounded. Our soldiers fought like tigers. It is considered almost certain that some of the enemy were hurt. Nothing definite is yet known. . . . But the fact is that the entire South is played out. Its armies have been reduced to almost nothing by desertion and disease. This is reliable. The following figures plainly show the facts in the case. Figures never lie:

Desertion per diem	100
" " month	3,000
For two years, as above,	312,000
Total of Lee's army, two years ago	300,000

> The balance have undoubtedly died in the hospitals, or been killed on the field. The result leaves Gen. Lee with twelve thousand men less than none. I don't quite understand it, but it is according to the statements of the newspaper correspondents generally, and therefore must be true. Their currency has depreciated so that a plate of cold ham would cost, in Richmond, two hundred and thirty dollars in gold. The only reason it doesn't, is that there isn't a plate of cold ham in Richmond. This is a fact.

Although a Union man and clearly on the winning side by this time, Arnold writes with a war-weariness that even imminent victory could not revive. This battle actually happened, but the report of Custer's actions are as ludicrous in their own right as the Falanx's fictitious one; and the jibe about ham in Richmond is not smugly triumphant, but part of a more elaborate sarcasm at the exaggerations of Union newspaper accounts of the war and "reliable" government assurances that "the entire South is played out." For George Arnold, war may not be hell, but it is certainly absurd.

◊ ◊ ◊

The popular press on both sides found plenty to satirize about the enemy's generals, and early in the war General Pierre Gustave Toutant Beauregard bore the brunt of this abuse for the South, General Benjamin Franklin Butler for the Union. (General George McClellan figured largely in popular humor and satire in the North as a presidential candidate in 1864.) Both sides, though, took shots at the officer corps generally. North or South, that humor reflects a fundamentally American affirmation of democratic good sense and distrust of authority: the common soldier, like the common man, respects real worth, not artificial rank.

Officers were easy targets for humor because they had real privileges, power, and social status that often comically contrasted with their vain-glorious show and downright incompetence. It was a common complaint in letters home, and in his widely reprinted poem (also put to music), "Says Private Maguire," Thomas Bailey Aldrich put that complaint in the down-home words of the common soldier—what would be appropriate for whatever cause he fought for.

> "*They* can go sparkin' and playin' at billiards,
> With greenbacks to spend for their slightest desire,
> Loafin' and atin', and dhrinkin' at Willard's [Hotel]
> While *we're* on the pickets," says Private Maguire.
> "Livin' in clover, they think it's a trifle
> To stand out all night in the rain and the mire,
> And a Rebel hard by with a villainous rifle,
> Jist ready to pop ye," says Private Maguire.

The foot soldier who showed himself superior to high and mighty officers was always humorous, of course, as in the story about Confederate General John Magruder dining well and alone in a Richmond restaurant. "He had hardly tested the merits of his repast when in sauntered a tall, long-haired, red-shirted private of the Louisiana First, which regiment had just arrived in the city. With the utmost coolness red-shirt sat himself down in the vacant chair opposite the General, and lit into the good things before him with a zest that plainly told of long marches and previous scanty rations." The general would have none of that. "'Sir, what do you mean?' he demanded. 'Do you know at whose table you are sitting?' The soldier, scarcely looking up, replied, in the interval between a bite and a drink, 'I know I am dreadful hungry; *and I ain't a bit particular who I eat with since I've gone soldiering.'*" This appeared in the "Editor's Drawer" column in *Harper's Monthly* (January 1864), but the butt of the humor there is not the Confederate general. He is a "brave officer and kind man," the opening sentence admits, "but filled with as much vanity, self-conceit, and pomposity as—as any general in the Federal army is." The satiric target, in other words, is any officer who presumes superiority over a soldiering private, particularly one who so coolly (and wittily) deflates a distinction so patently artificial.

An earlier version of the story, one with a pointedly different satirical hook, appeared in a Confederate newspaper, the *Memphis Daily Appeal* (2 November 1861). Here, the private is identified, the well-known Ned Phelps, who had just undergone a sixteen-hour march in the rain ordered by Magruder. *His* answer to the general's haughty question, therefore, is more personal: "'No! I don't know who I am eating with,' he replies, still helping himself from the general's plate, 'for since I cam [*sic*] soldiering I haven't been at all particular whom I eat with *so the victuals are clean.'*" Because Ned *would* have known the general, his comeback is all the more brazen and contemptuous of well-fed officers in an army of under-nourished privates, as the italicized words emphasize. (Later biographers of Magruder tell of the encounter with the general "delighted" by the response.)

A reader in *Southern Punch* (13 February 1864) did take the editor to task for being "too hard upon those whom you call 'the gold-braided gentry,'" but the fact is that in Confederate humor, disdain for officers, sometimes referred to along with non- combatants as "bombproofs," was more common and more bitter than it was in the Union. Class differences were greater and more historically entrenched in the South. Plantation owners could be immune from the draft, for example, and as the war continued, the phrase "Rich man's war, poor man's fight" resonated with conviction.

Signed by the "Foot Cavalry, From the privates of Alexander's Regt., 2nd Brigade," "Soldiers' Contemplation," in the *Clarksville (Texas) Standard* (9 January 1864), has its say with sarcasm founded in real experience.

> Of late I've oft been thinking of this great army-school,
> With iron regulations, and tyrants rigid rule.
> But chosen words, or phrases, I need no longer seek,
> Plain fact as soldiers know them, a stronger language speak.

Other verses record a litany of inequities. Officers get good food: "The Generals eat the poultry and buy it very cheap, / Our Colonels and our Captains, devour the hogs and sheep," while privates have to forage, and if caught are punished. "Sometimes we get so hungry we chance to steal a pig, / Then the biggest stump in Dixie, we're sure to have to dig." Plantation owners and officers, the "brass," on the other hand, not only lived well but did so at the expense of the lowly foot soldier.

> At every big plantation, or negro holder's yard,
> Just to save his property, the Generals place a guard.
> The sentry's then instructed to let no private pass,
> The rich man's house, and table are fixed to suit the brass.

The two-line chorus hammers home the injustice spelled out in each verse with the same rhetorical question: "Oh how'd you like the army, this high falutin army, / The brass-mounted army, where eagle buttons rule?"

One class of people knew even less than officers about the realities of war. It was "Very True," according to the title of a tersely poetic dialogue between two prominent, opposing generals published in *Southern Punch* (2 April 1864).

"John Halifax, Gent." solved a problem of the greatest moment, and sent it from "Camp" to the Charlottesville, Virginia, *Daily Chronicle*. Here it is:

> Quoth Meade to Lee,
> "Can you tell me,
> In the shortest style of writing,

When people will
Get their fill
Of this 'big job' of fighting?"

Quoth Lee to Meade,
"Why yes indeed,
I'll tell you in a minute;
When legislators,
And speculators,
Are made to enter in it."

In the North, Artemus Ward fulminated at length.

We don't, for instuns, lack great Gen'rals, and we certainly don't
lack brave sogers—but there's one thing I wish we did lack, and
that is our present Congress.

I venture to say that if you sarch the earth all over with a ten-
hoss power mikriscope, you won't be able to find such a pack of
poppycock gabblers as the present Congress of the United States
of America. . . .

Congress, you won't do. Go home you miserable devils—go
home! (1865, 35–36)

◊ ◊ ◊

War could be hellish, but soldiers spent only a fraction of their time
having at it with the enemy. Because most battles lasted less than a
week, soldiers spent most of their time in camp, and although safe,
life there was tedious. A page of cartoons in *Leslie's Budget of Fun* (June
1861) titled "The Romance and Reality of a Soldier's Life" illustrates the
gamut of what soldiering was all about, and that had more to do with
life in camp than in battle. The "romance" in the title is only implied,
a comic contrast to the pictures of the "reality of a soldier's life." A
writer in the *Charleston Mercury* (21 September 1861) put it in words
with ironic comparisons.

"The excitement of camp life." What a myth! Catch your young
birds with chaff, but don't try to sprinkle this sort of husk on the
tail of an old one. If you really want excitement, go to a Quaker
Meeting, attend a lecture on Phrenology, illustrated by the

"The Romance and Reality of a Soldier's Life." Courtesy of the Library Company of Philadelphia.

examination of [a] decrepit old gentleman's head, spend some Sunday afternoon in the fish market—these are lively and diverting amusements compared to the company, battalion and brigade drills—the breakfast, dinner and supper cooking—the noonday doze, the afternoon nap, the long uneasy night slumber—the dirt, the smoke, the heat the rain—which make up the sum of a camp day's unrelieved and intolerable tedium.

Young men with too much time on their hands did what they could to make the tedium more tolerable: sports and games, singing, gambling, writing letters, reading, music, and, of course, horseplay and practical jokes of all kinds that they shared in letters home. One joke took on a life of its own beyond the camp where it originated and became part of popular culture both printed and oral with the phrase, "Here's Your [sometimes 'Yer'] Mule." Claims to its origins vary, and although originally Confederate, it found its way north and was current long after the war.[4] It was a "popular phrase," the *Macon Telegraph* (26 October 1861) said, and Nashville music publisher C. D. Benson capitalized on that with the instrumental sheet music "Here's Your Mule Galop" in the same year.[5] (Another instrumental, "Here's Your Mule Schottische," was published in New Orleans early in 1862.)

The lyrics of the sheet music "Here's Your Mule, Comic Camp Song and Chorus," composed and published by C. D. Benson in Nashville and by John Church in Cincinnati in 1862, gave some clues about the practical joke that started it all. Announcing its performance on the Nashville stage, the *Nashville Dispatch* (21 June 1862) reported that "the laughable origin of the phrase, 'Here's yer mule,' is known to the generality of our readers, and these verses will be found in keeping with its humorous suggestions."

> A farmer came to camp one day
> With milk and eggs to sell,
> Upon a mule that oft would stray
> To where no one could tell.
> The farmer tired of his tramp
> For hours was made a fool,
> By ev'ryone he met in camp
> With "Mister, here's your mule!"
>
> Chorus: Come on, come on, come on, old man
> And don't be made a fool,

By ev'ry one you meet in camp
With "Mister, here's your mule!"

His eggs and chickens all were gone,
Before the break of day;
The mule was heard of all along,
That's what the soldiers say,
And still he hunted all day long,
Alas! a witless tool,
Whilst ev'ry man would sing the song,
Of, "Mister, here's your mule."

The soldiers run in laughing mood,
On mischief were intent;
They lifted muley on their back,
Around from tent to tent,
Thro' this hole and that, they pushed
His head and made a rule
To shout with hum'rous voices all,
"I say! Mister, here's your mule."

Alas, one day the mule was miss'd!
Ah! who could tell his fate?
The farmer like a man bereft,
Search'd early and search'd late,
And as he passed from camp to camp,
With stricken face—the fool,
Cried out to ev'ry one he met,
"Oh, Mister, where's my mule ?"

Sutlers, camp followers who peddled high-priced "necessities" to soldiers, were a common target for retaliatory jokes, but somehow, out of this one emerged a catchphrase that spread quickly as a broad, nonsensical sally for all kinds of unrelated occasions, including poetic parodies.[6]

Higher-ups did all they could, and that was a great deal, to keep the troops productively occupied and to remind them that they were, after all, soldiers. The standard text on both sides for military drills and tactics, *Hardee's Rifle and Light Infantry Tactics* (1855), furthered that effort with its numbingly detailed instructions, an open door to humor. A column titled "Hardee's Tactics Made Easy" appeared regularly in *Vanity Fair*, despite the lamely repetitive play on words, as in this: "In drilling

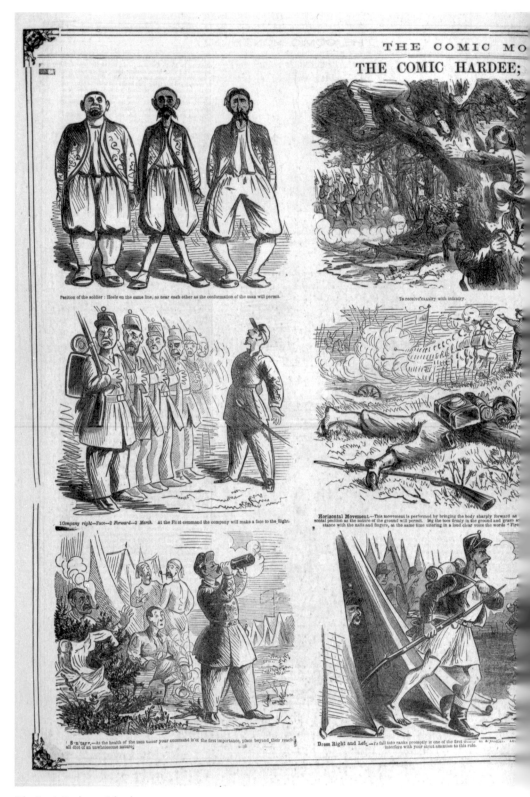

"The Comic Hardee; or School
of the Soldier." Courtesy of the
Library Company of Philadelphia.

To receive cavalry with Artillery.

Being in columns to break files.

Into Action.—In going into action protect your men as much as possible from the enemy's fire.

Prisoners.—In the hour of victory treat your prisoners humanely, but make them useful?

should always be provided with a good havelock. If the regiment does not supply them, he should procure one from home.

To advance on an Enemy in the Rear.—The length of the step will be eight or nine feet according as the conformation of the man will allow, and is swiftness at the rate of five hundred in a minute. Bring the foot sharply up with the toe pointed well forward—then go ahead.

recruits without Arms, it is not necessary to give them any instructions with regard to the disposal of their hands." The *Comic Monthly* (October 1861) did better with "The Comic Hardee: Or, School of the Soldier," two pages of twelve cartoons that contrast Hardee's stern nomenclature with the more realistic human behavior visually illustrated.

Col. John A. Godfrey, writing as "Gov.," made a serious effort to replace *Hardee's* with his *Rhymed Tactics* (1862) by translating the dry, military catechism of the original into what he believed an easier-to-learn because lighthearted verse—"To easy make the soldier's fate," as he wrote in the preface.

> I think you'll like my jingle.
> Camp life is dull and irksome, too,
> E'en for men stout and ruddy;
> But is aught worse to intersperse
> With toil than too much study? (Godfrey 1862, 1)

The instructions themselves, though, are no joke, with numbered paragraphs matching those in *Hardee's*, but Godfrey does his poetic best to lighten things up. *Hardee's* "official" paragraph #78 begins thus:

> Heels on the same line, as near each other as the conformation of the mail will permit;
> The feet turned out equally, and forming with each other something less than a right angle;
> The knees straight without stiffness
> The body erect on the hips, inclining a little forward;
> The shoulders square and falling equally.
> (Hardee 1861, 18–19)

In his commitment to make the soldier's fate more bearable, Godfrey renders Number #78 thusly:

> The heels on one line, and together as near
> As the size of your legs, or bowlegs will bear;
> The toes, turning out, while erect on the hip,
> Leaning forward a little—neither side tip—
> The body's adjusted. The shoulders keep square,
> Position as easy as home, or elsewhere.
> (1862, 19)

A lighthearted, even folksy effort as a spiced up alternative to the original, but few soldiers would have found 197 such paragraphs either entertaining or enlightening.

◊ ◊ ◊

The quip (attributed to Napoleon) that armies travel on their stomachs is not as powerful as Sheridan"s "War is Hell," but no less true, and all soldiers of all armies have complained about traveling that road. In the Civil War, griping about it regularly in letters home was often couched in pungent humor. A soldier from Alabama spun a tall tale about cows so emaciated that "it takes two hands to hold up one beef to shoot it"; an Ohio soldier wrote about meat so infested with maggots that "we had to have an extra gard to keep them from packing it clear off" (quoted in Wiley 1952, 249). At best, war meant dining that was "different," and soldiers soon created their own vocabulary for what they had to put up with, one that distinguished army rations from home fare. "Mess beef is 'salt horse,'" the *San Francisco Bulletin* (5 December 1861) reported in a story titled "New War Lingo": "Coffee is 'boiled rye,' vegetables are 'cow feed,' and butter is 'strong grease.'" The new vocabulary put such military provender in a comic place and at the same time created a grudging, comic camaraderie among those who had to suffer.

Complaints were real enough, but laughing at adversity always made it more tolerable. The song sheet "Dear Mother, I've Come Home to Eat" did that with a parody of the popular, deadly serious, "Dear Mother, I've Come Home to Die," both appearing appropriately together in *The Canteen Songster* (1865).

> Dear Mother, I remember well
> The food we get from Uncle Sam:
> Hard tack, salt junk, and rusty pork,
> Sometimes a scanty piece of ham.
> When I a furlough did receive,
> I bade adieu to Brother Pete—
> Oh! Mother, for a plate of hash.
> Dear Mother, I've come home to eat!
>
> Chorus: Oh for an hour at Meschutt's [Dining Room]
> I oft have dream'd when fast asleep;

> Stay, waiter, cod-fish balls for me,
> Dear Mother, I've come home to eat.

And this soldier knows exactly what he wants to eat when he gets home:

> I'm now content, no more I'll fight,
> Except it is a beef-steak rare;
> The army is no place for me.
> And shoddy isn't fit to wear.
> Oh! for some Quail from Jersey's woods,
> And Partridges with fixins neat.
> Dear Mother, that's my bill-of-fare.
> Dear Mother, I've come home to eat!

◊ ◊ ◊

Union sailors fared better, not only with superior provisions but with a regular ration of grog, a medicinal carryover from British naval practice. Until 1 September 1862, that is, when the rum and water was stopped. Composed the month before by Caspar Schenk, U.S.N., "Farewell to Grog" mourned the loss with humor, all the more so by adapting an English drinking song for the occasion.

> Come, messmates pass the bottle round
> Our time is short, remember,
> For our grog must stop and our spirits drop
> On the first day of September.
>
> Chorus: For tonight we'll merry, merry be
> For tonight we'll merry, merry be
> For tonight we'll merry, merry be
> Tomorrow we'll be sober.

Foot soldiers would not have been sympathetic. For them, hardtack (biscuits made with flour, water, and salt) came to stand for everything they had to endure when it came to army food. A bread substitute, hardtack was fairly nourishing and virtually indestructible, but the latter, not the former, made for wry laughs. Under the title "Antiquity of Army Crackers," the *Leavenworth (Kansas) Daily Times* (17 November

1861) quoted a letter from a Colonel McLean, complaining, "The crackers we eat are stamped '1801,' and the boys say they have seen several marked 'B. C.'" (A good joke, but the "boys" would have known, even if civilians would not, that "B. C." stood for "Brigade Commissary.") If moisture got to the biscuits, infesting them with bugs, the boys joked about finally getting some "meat."

In "Hard Tack" (see plate 7), one in Winslow Homer's second series of souvenir chromo cards titled "Life in Camp" (1864), the exaggerated size of the cracker, like the soldier's expression, gives a comically visual sense of what it was like to gag one down.

What has endured as the most widely known complaint about this staple of military nourishment is the song "Hard Crackers, Come Again No More," sung to the Stephen Foster song "Hard Times, Come Again No More" (1855).[7]

> Let us close our game of poker,
> Take our tin cups in hand,
> While we gather round the cook's tent door
> Where dry mummies of hard crackers
> Are given to each man;
> Oh, hard crackers come again no more!
>
> Chorus: 'Tis the song and the sigh of the hungry,
> Hard crackers, hard crackers, come again no more!
> Many days have you lingered upon our stomachs sore,
> Oh, hard crackers, come again no more.

◊ ◊ ◊

As with other parodies of this kind, there was fun to be had in the contrast to the solemn words of the original and its familiar tune, as well as singing the parody along with fellow sufferers. "When the cry of fall in for your bread rung out, you ought to have seen the boys hop out, some of them singing, 'Hard tack! hard tack! come again no more,'" a Wisconsin soldier reported in the *Madison (Wisconsin) Daily Patriot* (17 February 1863).

Union soldiers felt the pinch of few and barely palatable rations, but did so temporarily and locally. For Confederate soldiers, as with civilians, the shortage of provender was not just systemic but endemic and worsened as war continued. A. E. Blackmar published the sheet music "Goober Peas" in New Orleans after the war, in 1866, but it has all of the earmarks of a wartime camp song.[8] Rations for the "Georgia militia," according to the third stanza, have been reduced to goobers, "peanuts," but these soldiers will not be daunted. Even the title page is playful, crediting the words to "P. Nutt," the music to "A. Pindar." ("Pindar," like "goober," is an African American word for "peanut.")

> Sitting by the roadside on a summer day,
> Chatting with my messmates, passing time away,
> Lying in the shadow underneath the trees,
> Goodness, how delicious, eating Goober Peas!
>
> Chorus: Peas! peas! peas! peas! eating Goober Peas!
> Goodness how delicious, eating Goober Peas!

Sung to a rollicking tune, the ironic bravado of the words is lost to most people now who hear or who sing it as a celebration of peanuts. Lost as well is an affective longing for the end of war that has nothing to do with defeatism or cowardice:

> I think my song has lasted almost long enough,
> The subject's interesting, but rhymes are mighty rough,
> I wish this war was over, when free from rags and fleas,
> We'd kiss our wives and sweethearts and gobble Goober
>   Peas!

The sheet music "Short Rations" (1864) is too arcane to be widely sung today, but it has more to say about circumstances in the Confederacy at the time and the ways that humor dealt with them. Overtly, it is a response to yet another reduction in army rations, this time in Tennessee, but the first verse has a much broader indictment, addressing everyone—all non-combatants (as well as certain officers)—who should listen to this "song of starvation!"

> Fair ladies and maids of all ages,
> Little girls and cadets how e'er youthful,
> Home guards, quartermasters and sages,
> Who write for the newspapers so truthful!
> Clerks, Surgeons and Supes, Legislators,
> Staff Officers (fops of the nation),

"Short Rations." Courtesy of the Lester S. Levy Collection, The Sheridan Libraries, The Johns Hopkins University.

    And even you dear speculators,
    Come list to my song of starvation!

This is serious business at heart, as are the other verses, which the cover comically relieves so very well and at the same time so very poignantly. "Not satisfied," says the mule at the empty trough, its sides chewed away, the animal a comic stand-in for soldiers whose only ration by this time in the conflict is corn.

    The "Corn-Fed" is proof to all evils,
    Has a joke for all hardships and troubles,
    In honor and glory he revels,
    Other fancies he looks on as bubbles!
    He is bound to be free, and he knows it,
    Then what cares he for toil and privation!
    He is brave, and in battle he shows it,
    And will conquer in spite of starvation.

Despite "starvation," "toil," and "privation," the "Corn-fed" not only endures but prevails and does so with humorous defiance, "a joke for all hardships and troubles."

Whether rations for soldiers were, in fact, reduced to corn in Tennessee (or to peanuts in Georgia), "Short Rations" (like "Goober Peas") is about real, fundamental problems of the Confederacy, problems that the Union did not face. Federal soldiers griped about hardtack, but they usually fared better, and hard crackers had something to do with the incompetence of military higher-ups, not with a nation ravaged. Underlying much Confederate humor about the war, especially in the last two years, lay a sense of a nation not yet defeated by an outside enemy but inexorably enervated by war itself. Humor could acknowledge that without defeatism or cowardice, evoking laughter that was perhaps fatalistic but nonetheless defiant—"absurdist" in the modern, existential sense of that term. That is the gist of the playful pseudonyms for the composer, "Ye Tragic," and the lyricist, "Ye Comic," on the cover of "Short Rations."[9]

Chapter Four

THE AFRICAN AMERICAN IN CIVIL WAR HUMOR

Before the Civil War, in both the North and South, blackface minstrelsy—and not only theater performances but also the playbills, songsters, sheet music, and broadsides that they generated—had fixed in the popular imagination the conventions for how the African American (almost exclusively male) would be delineated in humor by and for whites during the war itself. Physically, he looked comically grotesque, with large lips and teeth, woolly hair, a wide nose, and big feet with an elongated heel. The most clearly identifying aspect of the caricature, on stage and in print, was a way of speaking that included comic malapropisms, odd speech mannerisms of various kinds, and above all a dialect, a simplistic inventory of bad grammar and peculiar pronunciations. Cartoons, sheet music covers, pictorial envelopes, and lithographs illustrated the stereotyped physical features, but the most popular forms were songs, speeches, and sermons in which the caricature spoke in the distinctive blackface dialect that made the character "authentic" to whites and, therefore, made what he said appear as a legitimately black perspective on a variety of issues.

The African American appeared less often in Confederate humor and usually with none of the coarse, unabashed racism often found in the Union. In the South, after all, slavery was a benevolent institution; slaves were happy there, and even those who had "runned away" were used as comic foils that made the satiric case against wrongheaded, hypocritical Northerners. In Union humor, the figure appeared prominently, as it had before the war (because there, race *as* race was contentious), in response to new issues that the war raised. For example, few in the Union advocated abolition—and they did not do so humorously—but during the war the slave caricature could be turned into a good laugh at an enemy painted broadly, and inaccurately, as slave masters. Victory, therefore, would mean the end of slavery. For Peace Democrats, on the other hand, the black caricature provided a comically ironic voice against the war and those who supported it, painted broadly, and inaccurately, as abolitionists. All of this had much to do with either war-mongering propaganda or political posturing (or both) and very little to do with "real" black Americans. In the course of the war, though, two events forced a serious rethinking of their place in the political, economic, and social life of the North—in the ultimately "united states," which was, after all, the Union cause for taking up arms. The first event, in 1861, was the official designation of blacks as "contrabands," slaves who crossed Union lines; the second was that section of the Emancipation Proclamation in 1863 authorizing the recruitment of black soldiers.

◊ ◊ ◊

While few in the North had high-minded convictions about emancipation, the slave caricature was ideally suited for twitting the Confederate enemy in a variety of comic ways. "The Rebellion's Support" in the *Comic Monthly* (January 1862) did it with a full-page cartoon. Literally, the diminutive, belligerent Confederate and the slave culture he defends are in the palm of Pompey's hand. On the other hand, figuratively, the slave who dominates the cartoon does so comically with his stereotypical, Negroid appearance and is not to be taken seriously as a person who should be free. The exaggerations of caricature do make the slave's triumph over his master all the more satiric.

Dialect alone could do that. A mock advertisement in *Leslie's Illustrated Newspaper* (11 January 1862) from one Sambo Rhett of Beaufort, South Carolina, for his runaway owner parodies the announcements for escaped slaves that regularly appeared in newspapers before the war.

$500 Reward.—Rund away from me on de 7th of dis month [November 1861], my massa Julan Rhett. Massa Rhett am five feet 'leven inches high, big shoulders, brack har, curly shaggy whiskers,

THE REBELLION'S SUPPORT.—Pompey.—"I'se holdin' ye up now, but wouldn't I drop ye quick, ef Uncle Sam 'd ony gib de word."

"The Rebellion's Support." Courtesy of the Library Company of Philadelphia.

low forehead and dark face. He make big fuss when he go 'mong
de gemmen, he talk ver big, and use de name of de Lord all ob de
time. Calls heself "Suddern gemmen," but I suppose will try now to
pass heself off as a brack man or mulatter. Massa Rhett has a deep
scar on his shoulder from a fight, scratch 'cross de left eye, made
by my Dinah when he tried to whip her. He neber look people in
de face.

A parody, but it goes further in playing up wartime stereotypes of
slave-owning "Suddern gemmen" in the Northern popular imagination. Readers then would have been amused too by the name "Massa
Rhett," knowing that firebrand secessionist of long-standing, Robert
Barnwell Rhett, of Beaufort, South Carolina, had led the state as the
first to leave the Union.

The humor of this kind of reversal has everything to do with the
black voice used by whites, because that voice most clearly identi-
fies the speaker *as* black and therefore ratchets up the ironic turn of
events. A grinning slave pictured lounging in a hammock, languidly
strumming a banjo in "A New Plantation Song" in *Vanity Fair* (5 March
1862) illustrates that reversal well enough, but his dialect rubs it in—
"Brack folks turn has come, dat's so!"—and adds an insulting tone to
his derision of the flag that waved over the new nation:

> Here's de rag with seven stars
> Massa toted to de wars
> To scare de Yankee Nation
> Now boys, three times three Yah! Yah!
> For the rebel spots and bars
> Nebermore to wave—no *Sars*!

"Obsequies of the Southern Confederacy, Sermon by Rev. William
Bones," in *Frank Leslie's Budget of Fun* (May 1862), has all of the conventions of the comic sermon popularized on the antebellum minstrel
stage—the good reverend mangles vocabulary and grammar with
impassioned abandon—but here that way of speaking is used to reduce
the ultimate demise of the Confederacy to a laughable certainty. It
"has widered away and faded like de baseless fabrick ob a nightmare,"
he exhorts; it has "squashed, caved in, used up, cleared out, kicked de
bucket an' gone in! Hope 'twon't neber come out again."

The most popular comic treatment of the reversal of slave and master might be Henry Clay Work's song "Kingdom Coming," published
with great fanfare and instant success in April 1862, reprinted many
times as a broadside, and sung on the minstrel stage. The chorus
trumpets the message of what will happen when Union troops head
south—"De massa run, ha, ha! De darkey stay, ho, ho!"—and each
verse gives the details of a world turned upside down.

> Say, darkies, hab you seen de massa, wid de muffstash on his
>   face,
> Go long de road some time dis mornin', like he gwine to leab
>   de place?
> He seen a smoke way up de ribber, whar de Linkum gunboats
>   lay;
> He took his hat, and lef' berry sudden, and I spec' he's run
>   away!
>
> He six foot one way, two foot tudder, and he weigh tree hun-
>   dred pound,
> His coat so big, he couldn't pay the tailor, an' it won't go half-
>   way round.
> He drill so much dey call him Cap'n, an' he got so drefful
>   tanned,
> I spec' he try an' fool dem Yankees for to tink he's
>   contraband.
>
> De darkeys feel so lonesome libbing in de loghouse on de
>   lawn,
> Dey move dar tings into massa's parlor for to keep it while
>   he's gone.
> Dar's wine an' cider in de kitchen, an' de darkeys dey'll have
>   some;
> I s'pose dey'll all be cornfiscated when de Linkum sojers come.
>
> De oberseer he make us trouble, an' he dribe us round a spell;
> We lock him up in de smokehouse cellar, wid de key trown in
>   de well.
> De whip is lost, de han'cuff broken, but de massa'll hab his
>   pay;

He's ole enough, big enough, ought to known better dan to
went an' run away.

As in the mock advertisement for the "rund away massa," the "darky"
dialect makes the description of the Cavalier slave owner all the more
irreverent, magnified here with the uprooting of plantation life and
the newly empowered slaves taking over the now-vacant master's
house and locking up the "oberseer." The ultimately ironic reversal is
all about the master, who "got so drefful tanned" that he could evade
capture, "passing," as it were, as a slave.

Given what seems a clear enough message in Work's popular song,
it had a paradoxical appeal at the time and a checkered history after.
The words are not passionately antislavery, but Work *was* an abolitionist, and his song was sung by the Hutchinson Family, a popular singing troupe with a repertoire so radical that a Union general once for-
bade them from entertaining his troops. On the other hand, Christy's
Minstrels premiered it on stage, Bryant's Minstrels performed it, and
neither troupe had any commitment to emancipation. So too, surely,
the thousands who bought the sheet music and would have enjoyed
singing about the vivid and literal overturning of the master's table
with little thought to Work's deeper meaning. Most curious is its publication in the heart of the Confederacy, Augusta, Georgia, in 1864, "as
sung by the First Tennessee Opera Group," the title page announced.
Perhaps this was another manifestation late in the war of that Confederate sensibility that acknowledged a bitter reality with ironic humor.
This version, however, does moderate the full effect of the original by
tempering the black dialect some and omitting the last verse about
the "oberseer," the profoundly evil embodiment of slavery indelibly
stamped in the popular imagination by Harriet Beecher Stowe's characterization of Simon Legree in her best-selling 1852 novel, *Uncle Tom's
Cabin*. More understandable is that black troops reportedly sang the
song as they marched into Richmond in April 1865, that black minstrels performed it after the war, and that it became part of the black
oral tradition.[1]

African Americans would not be enlisted until 1863, but the minstrel mask served earlier in the Union cause as a kind of cracker-barrel
reporter who could put a comic spin on bad news for the Union. "You
may talk about de times, / But jes listen to my rhymes: / It brings you
de news accordin'," says the speaker in the song sheet "Happy Land of
Canaan No. 5."

Oh the Rebels they can blow,
As all ob you may know,
Kase dey beat us at de battle of Bull-Run;
But when we come on dem again,
We shall show dem some fun,
And bring dem to de happy land of Canaan.

In each chorus, he takes aim at the Confederate president:

De peple in de South am getting mighty hot
But afore dey know, old Jeff will get a shot
Dat will send him to de happy land of Canaan.

Ginger Jim, in "Ginger Jim's Union Cockade," admits that the Union had faltered early on, but he salutes Union victories in New Orleans and at Pittsburg Landing, Tennessee (now called the battle of Shiloh).

Dis war commenced at Sumter,
And dey gib de Union beans,
But soon dey had de Stars and Stripes
To wave ober New Orleans;
For since de fight at Pittsburg,
It's goin' such a way,
Dat Union's bound to win, my boys,
No matter what you say.

The chorus is a rousing cheer for flagging white hearts: "Shout, boys, shout, and don't you be afraid / To sport de feathers in your hat, de Union cockade."

The 1862 broadside "The New Jim Crow" is the most imaginative, most elaborate adaptation of earlier minstrel material to the war. Created by Thomas "Daddy" Rice in 1828, Jim Crow was the first popular blackface character and the title of the signature song of Rice's performance that appeared in different versions and a variety of broadside forms and sheet music over the years. With as many as sixty-six verses, the original is a hodgepodge of minstrel stage "business" but is essentially a "political song," Dale Cockrell says (1977, 73), with plainspoken opinions on Andrew Jackson's battle with the United States Bank and on the Nullification Crisis in 1832, a prelude to the constitutional crisis of the Civil War for which African Americans could and would fight.

> Should dey get to fighting,
> Perhaps de blacks will rise,
> For deir wish for freedom,
> Is shining in deir eyes.
> An if de blacks should get free,
> I guess dey'll feel some bigger,
> An I shall consider it,
> A bold stroke for de nigger.

A radical notion for an apparent black man, although, as Eric Lott writes, "Like most of the potentially subversive moments of early minstrelsy, they are qualified by 'darky' dialect (in the theatre and orthographic derision)" (1993, 24).

"The New Jim Crow" is an update of the original—"About the Darkies and the War," the subtitle says—and while this Crow's style is informal, even folksy, no dialect or orthography "qualifies," in Lott's sense, his candid opinions. The forty-four verses take on a wide range of targets. Like Ginger Jim and other black patriots, he celebrates Union victories, pokes fun at an incompetent Rebel army, and disdains the Confederate president, but he goes further with a derisive dismissal of the kinds of arguments long used to justify slavery.

> CONSTITUTIONAL: "If the darkies are not persons, tell me why, you dixie men, / When you elect for Congress you make darkies persons then."
> BIBLICAL: "The dixies pick out scripture to prove that slav'rys right, / But they do make a bad mistake—that shows they'r not so bright."
> SCIENTIFIC: "The dixies say the darkey's head for learning is not fit; / But they wont let him try to learn; they fear he has the wit."

Several verses are given to each argument, each two-line verse hammered home by the familiar refrain that signaled the shuffling dance that Rice had made famous on stages throughout American and England:

> So I wheel about,
> I turn about,
> I do just so,
> And every time I wheel about,
> I jump Jim Crow.

Dan Rice had made the words famous, but this Jim Crow gives them new meaning, a "turn about" indeed.

Peace Democrats, on the other hand, used the blackface persona to make the very different argument that the war was a mistake and not in the best interests of blacks. Byron Christy delivered "Dat's What's de Matter" with the dialect, malapropisms, non sequiturs, and general nonsense of the minstrel stump speech, but beneath the animated comic trappings lay a serious message.

> But, feller citizens, if you don't want the fraternal viscera ob yer animal system riddled like a sieve, by de worms ob remorse, preserve de Union! If yer don't want yer spinal column ob yer backbone made a rat road fur de grim and gory goblins ob despair, preserve de Union! If you don't want de American Eagle plucked bare as a New-Year's turkey, preserve de Union! And if you want de Stars and Stripes to wave aloft, and flounce, and do just as it dam pleases—preserve de Union and save yer country."

Who better to stump for peace at any price than an African American, who, one would think, should benefit from the war? Who takes no side, apparently, finding fault with "white folks" South as well as North, as "Eph" does in the 1862 sheet music "Young Eph's Lament."

> Oh, I wish dat de white folks of dis great confederation
> Would only quit dar quarrels and dar fight;
> And stop dar cannonading, marching, shooting, and
>   bombarding,
> And be willing for to use each oder right.

"Saucy Sam," in a song sheet of the same name, was more emphatic:

> If I was de President, I'd take a bold position:
> I'd play de very deuce wid dat nigger Abolition;
> I'd make secession hold its jaw, and 'Mancipation, too,
> And I'd make 'em cry out: Union! as Washington used to do.

Sam and, apparently, the white author miss the ironic humor of his being president.

As outlandish as President Sam and others like him sound today given his sentiments, and would to many people in the 1860s, they were the humorous, blackface counterparts to the dour Copperhead editorials that raged against the war as an abolitionist conspiracy. In a different kind of ironic reversal—and intended to be humorous for that reason—*these* slaves condemned a war for emancipation, a point of view made all the more credible by admitting to the inhumane treatment that abolitionists had long denounced. Saucy Sam admits that "his master used to whallop" him, but he speaks for reconciliation, not a Union victory that would mean the end of slavery. So, too, Pompey Moore, from the "ole Virginny shore" (place names gave the speakers plausibility), and in the song sheet "Pompey Moore" he admits that he "neber had any education / Except now and den a lickin' / Down at de cotton-pickin'," but he wants nothing to do with freedom.

> Let Abolition die,
> And Secession keep shy,
> And de Norf and de Souf shake hands;
> And now, white folks, hear me:
> Just leave de nigger be,
> For, I tell you dey isn't worth a cent.

If a slave could say such things, the white authors seem to say, how could any white person, even an abolitionist, say them nay?

The speaker in "Topsey's Doctrine" is one of the few black female figures in Civil War humor, one that readers would have connected to Topsy, the young slave in *Uncle Tom's Cabin* whose lot in life improved when a female Yankee do-gooder spirited her away to the North. This "Topsey" turns that upside down with her impudent embracing of life on the plantation, "dancing jigs" and "cutting up all sorts of rigs." Unlike the mopey Pompey Moore, she bubbles with life and, with a witty play on words, has a different sense of her "worth."

> But I cannot quite exactly see
> What I should gain by liberty;
> For I am worth, just as I stand,
> A thousand dollars cash in hand!
> So as a slave I'll be content,
> 'Cause free niggers isn't worth a cent.

◊ ◊ ◊

Whether speaking for or against the war and the Union, none of these characterizations reckoned seriously with the real person of the African American; whites used the blackface mask as one of many weapons in a war of words and pictures. The conventions of that caricature did not change, but two events did abruptly alter the status of African Americans and compel a more serious, often ambiguous and therefore often comic, re-examination of their new place in American culture North and South.

In May 1861, a month after the fall of Sumter, blacks themselves set that re-examination in motion when slaves escaped from their owners and sought refuge in Fort Monroe, Virginia, a Union toehold in the Confederacy, commanded by General Benjamin Butler. Because they were "property" in the South, he declared them "contrabands of war," refused to send them back to a seceded state, and put them to work on Union fortifications. Confederates fumed, but it cheered most Northerners, who, although they cared little for the plight of slaves, saw their flight as another blow against the Confederacy.[2] The preface to a two-page spread of etchings of contrabands titled "Negroes Taking Refuge at Fort Monroe," in *Frank Leslie's Illustrated Newspaper* (8 June 1861), summed up the situation: "The promptness and sagacity of General Butler have increased the dilemma of the Secessionists to a remarkable degree, since it is at once equally hostile to both Abolitionism and Secession." In the following months and years, tens of thousands of slaves slipped over to the Union along a line of hundreds of miles, but "Fortress Monroe" was the symbolic port of entry. In the 1861 lithograph titled "The (Fort) Monroe Doctrine," with an image that appeared in other genres, slaves dash for safety to the fort, the one in the foreground thumbing his nose at the whip-wielding former master, a caricature of hatchet-faced, goateed Southerner Jefferson Davis, the living embodiment of the Confederacy. Most Southerners did not own slaves, of course, but the flood of contrabands denied the Confederacy an important resource and represented for the Union an early symbolic victory that made for some fun at a time when the war was not going well. The first battle at Bull Run, in July 1861, the first major battle in the war, for example, was a disaster for the North, but a pictorial envelope turned it into something of a victory over the F.F.V. (First Family of Virginia), given the desertion of some former slaves (see plate 8). And while Butler did put escaped slaves to work, another envelope shows a contraband more than happy with what to him is freedom with his new "Massa."

Whereas Northern propaganda depicted contrabands as laboring contentedly for the Union, the Confederate press portrayed them as regretting their decision to head North. In "The Returned Prodigal,"

"The (Fort) Monroe Doctrine."
Courtesy of the American
Antiquarian Society.

"By golly Massa Butler. I like dis better dan workin' in de field for ole Secesh massa." Courtesy of
the Collection of the New-York Historical Society.

SOUTHERN PUNCH.

THE RETURNED PRODIGAL.

DINAH.—Great sakes alive! Cum back from de Yankees?

SAMBO.—Yes, mighty glad to git back to marster. De Ole Boy down to Norfolk, he call heself Butler, but I knows dat he cum from below. One eye looks up to Hebben as it he is watchin what is doin up dare; tother eye looks down to de pocket, watchin what's dare. He is monstrous hard on black folks. It was work, work, all de time, and so I runs away and cums home.

PUNCHIANA.

Why is sorrow like a spoiled child? Because if you do not nurse it, it will

Why does liquor as it increases in price become more dangerous? Because it puts so many men upon their bier (beer)

What class of persons are the most anxious to rise? They that stoop the lowest.

"The Returned Prodigal." Courtesy of The Library of Virginia.

Fate of the Contrabands.

PAT—What am I to do with the Nagers ?

YANK—Look here, mister; I guess any one who places himself under the Starry Banner of the free, will have to work; out of the ranks and in the ranks, for that blessed privilege—'specially if he's a nigger. You must cum down on these contrabands-like-a-hull team, and make 'em dig and drill Butler and Banks and the-rest of the Generals have sed it, and more than all, Old Abe has swore it. Guess sum of the darkies wish themselves to hum ; but they won't git there till they do their duty to their new masters.

"Fate of the Contrabands." Courtesy of The Library of Virginia.

in *Southern Punch* (2 January 1864), Sambo has had enough of General Butler, "De Ole Boy down to Norfolk." Confederate propagandists also used the occasion to skewer Yankee hypocrites, as *Southern Punch* (26 December 1863) did in "Fate of the Contrabands." Confederate propaganda did not condemn slaves for making the misguided decision to head north; doing so would have implicitly acknowledged that they were better off there, contrary to the hoary argument that they lived happily and were treated more benignly in the South, "to hum," as popular literature would have it.

Peace Democrats in the North made much the same argument but played up the fate of the former slave in what for them was a political salvo against anybody who supported the war, which is to say, abolitionists, very generally speaking. In the song sheet "The Contraband's Adventures," "Darkey Sam" gives a firsthand account of what happened in the North when he fell into the hands of no-good do-gooders who did their best to make him white.

> Dey got me very soon,
> And dey put me in a room:
> Dis nigger couldn't tell what dey was arter;
> Dey took off all my clothes,
> And den what does you suppose?
> Dey put me in a tub of boilin water!

Nothing works, of course—soap, sandpaper, and lime—and Sam survives the ordeal to deliver a sage message to abolitionists:

> Gemmen, list to me,
> And you will find out dat I am right, man;
> De nigger will be nigger,
> Till de day of Jubilee;
> For, he nebber was intended for a white man;
> Den just skedaddle home,
> Leave de colored man alone;
> For, you're only makin' trouble for de nation.

The author asks for no sympathy for Sam's treatment; we are supposed to find it funny, an example of abolitionist idiocy and what Sam deserves for going North.

The slave in the broadside "The Contraband's Lament," who "just come from de Souf to St. Louis," on the other hand, was well received. The people "dey all seem quite enchanted wid my face," he says, "and de ladies, in particular, say I'm cupid, don't you see?" Despite it all, though, this black man knows where he belongs (ironically, the "lament" in the title?): "But dis gay and easy life is not suitable for me, / For I was raised a nigger, and a nigger still must be." Maybe such convictions, apparently by the contrabands themselves, gave solace to some readers—contrabands would literally go away and, figuratively, so would the problems they posed—but the author concludes with a warning to those who would see it differently.

> So, white folks, let me tell you, before I do depart,
> Don't let de cause of niggers so encircle round your heart:
> We are over four millions now in numbers, don't you see?
> And what could you do wid all of us, if we were all set free?

◊ ◊ ◊

"What could you do?" That, indeed, was the question. Many of the fictional contrabands in popular humor had the good sense to go back to the plantation, figments of white imaginations. It created a convenient way for Northerners to have some fun at the expense of the Confederacy, but the thousands of former slaves who crossed the line also created new and troubling social and economic problems for the Union. The *Leavenworth (Kansas) Daily Times* (21 December 1861) prefaced its sober reporting of the matter with the question, "What's to Be Done with Them?"

> One hundred and five contrabands, of all ages, sexes and conditions, arrived in the city yesterday in every stage of destitution and want. They formed a most dismal procession down Shawnee street, and their faces exhibited anything but a contented look. They were quartered somewhere in town last evening. The rapid increase of this class in our midst may well suggest the query— "What shall be done with them?"

One answer was to make a joke of the situation, as in "Dark Artillery; Or, How to Make the Contrabands Useful" in *Frank Leslie's Illustrated Newspaper* (26 October 1861).

Again, the conventional response was to blame the problem on abolitionists, a term used loosely for those who wanted to end slavery (as in "The Contraband's Adventures" above) but who were accused of avoiding the consequences. Although not in fact an abolitionist, as the editor of the *New York Tribune*, the unofficial voice of Radical Republicanism, Horace Greeley made a convenient target. "The Highly Intelligent Contraband, Who Has Come All the Way from 'Down South' to

DARK ARTILLERY; OR, HOW TO MAKE THE CONTRABANDS USEFUL.

"Dark Artillery; or, How to
Make the Contrabands Useful."
Courtesy of the American
Antiquarian Society.

Visit Mr. Greeley, but Horace 'Doesn't See It!'" in *Vanity Fair* (26 April
1862), is more artfully drawn than most cartoons. Except for his right
foot, someone is seen fleeing only in shadow, but that shadowy profile
would have been recognizable as the tempestuous editor. The starkly
drawn contraband, on the other hand, arrests the eye; he is visually
"Negroid" in the sense of the time, and only the laughable flight of
Greeley mitigates the implicit threat of his club and the aggressive,
resolute stance of this "intelligent contraband."

The term "intelligent contraband" had a different meaning from
the more general "contraband." First used, along with "reliable contraband," by journalists to describe slaves who provided "intelligence"
about the enemy, it turned ironic in the popular media. For the satiric
point that the *Vanity Fair* cartoon wants to make, the black *is* intelligent enough to come a long ways to seek out Greeley, but the visual
caricature assures that he is not, really. Ironic, too, is the speaker in

"The Highly Intelligent
Contraband." Courtesy of Special
Collections/Musselman Library,
Gettysburg College.

"The Intelligent Contraband," a comic song that "has been successful in Ethiopian concerts in Boston," according to *Dwight's Journal of
Music* (30 September 1865).

> I is de happiest darkiee
> Dat ever you did see.
> I've been so ever since I heard
> Dat I was to be free.
>
> I was born way down in Dixie's land
> Dey use to call me Sam,
> Bi, Golly! now de white folks say
> I'm a 'telligent contraband.

With their usual rigor and vigor, Radical Democrats invoked more
dire consequences for what some people might "do" with droves of
escaped slaves. They excoriated Republicans who "planned to feed,
house, clothe, and educate the emancipated slave with the white man's
money," Forrest G. Wood writes in *The Black Scare*, "and leave the needy
whites to shift for themselves" (1970, 24). Crediting the *Logan (Ohio)
Gazette* with the poem "De United States Hotel," the *Columbus (Ohio)
Crisis* (18 June 1862) said it was "too good to lay over—send it round."
And it was, appearing in Peace Democrat newspapers from New York
to Wisconsin over the following months, another comic alternative to
editorial tirades on the subject. This contraband wants nothing to do
with going back home; the mollycoddling he gets at the United States
Hotel (also called Uncle Sam's Hotel) suits him and the other boarders
just fine.

> And don't you know de boardahs?—de accomplished Dinah
>   Crow—
> De scrushinatin' Pompey, and de gallant Mistah Snow—
> And all ob de "born equals," no matter whar dey dwell,
> Are goin' to be boardahs at Uncle Sam's Hotel.

With lip-smacking detail, he relishes the good life they will all have
living free at the expense of whites:

> De scrushinatin' Pompey, when he sits down to dine,
> Just hear him call de waitah, to fotch along de wine!

> And see de little white boys a helpin' Mistah' Snow,
> And bringing chicken fixin's to de lubly Dinah Crow.

In case anyone has missed the point, the last stanza hammers home what will happen if escaped slaves are allowed to run rampant in the Union.

> Oh take the mattock, white man!—de shubbel and de
>   spade—
> We boardahs hab no work to do, we all hab quit de trade!
> But 'fore you pay de boahd bills, you'll hab to tug and sweat,
> And wish you wan't white trash a thousand times, I'll bet.

Spoken by a black voice in 1862, the term "white trash" would have been as offensive to whites as the word "nigger" is to blacks today when used by whites. As the writer intended, of course, it was part of the consequences of emancipation, as he saw it, enumerated so enthusiastically by the free-loading contraband himself.

Such unabashed racism, however, was the work of Copperhead editors and their readers, "a distinct and often hopeless minority," Wood says (1970, 38), but "The Contraband's Hotel" did move into mainstream popular culture in different and curious ways that would seem to say something (but what?) about the dynamics of Civil War humor—who laughed at what and why.

Many in the Confederacy had their own kind of fun with the story in the 1862 publication in Nashville of the sheet music "The Contraband's Hotel," attributed to J. Rud Adam, and its performance on stage there. Their enjoyment, though, probably had less to do with Union politics and more with a good turnabout laugh at Northerners who had such great fun with runaway slaves thumbing their noses at their masters. Frank Wilder took credit for the same words to a different tune in the sheet music "Uncle Sam's Hotel," issued by a prominent music publisher in Boston, Oliver Ditson. Boston was not a hotbed of War Democrats, so there must have something entertaining about singing in black dialect with friends and family. In Philadelphia in 1863, J. E. Gould published yet another sheet music version, again with different music but also very different words. This version takes the title of the newspaper poem, "De United States Hotel, by One of De Boardahs," but this contraband repudiates what it says with a virtual line-by-line parody. He poses no threat to white society, no arrogant presumption

SOUTHERN PUNCH.

Back to "Ould Ireland."

YANKEE.—Bridget, I guess we will not require your services next month, as I have engaged the services of a colored cook from the South.

BRIDGET.—Bad luck to you and the nagers; sure divil a bit do I care; I'll go back to Ireland where a white girl is better than a black nagur.

Cured of Gaming.

nerius. Since then, I saw that a gambler

"Back to 'Ould Ireland.'" Courtesy of The Library of Virginia.

of "born equals," but "scap'd darkies"; "White boys" don't wait on "Mistah Snow," but "the little niggah" does, he says, and the only trash is "de Souf trash." And most important, *these* contraband will do their part and work with gusto: "Gib *us* de mattock, white man, de shubbel and de spade / We boardahs hab de work to do, we'll nebber quit de trade." Taken by itself, the language reads as racist to the modern ear, but here it gives credibility to a very different racial ideology from the original Copperhead verses, one voiced enthusiastically by the white folks who sang it. (These lyrics also appeared in three song books published by Beadle and Company in 1864, 1865, and 1879.)

◊ ◊ ◊

If contraband did want to work, though, what to do with that new labor force of millions? As would-be president "Saucy Sam" quoted earlier put it, "I don't like abolitionists, to please a foolish whim, / Shove poor white folks out of work, and put de nigger in." Wood argues that "the economic burden of emancipation—possibly excluding the loss of the slave owner's investment—was relatively insignificant" (1970, 24). Copperhead publicists, however, sniffing political victory in the 1864 election, brought racial and class tensions to a boil in many Union cities, targeting the large Irish working class who would be allegedly displaced by blacks. The cartoon "Back to 'Ould Ireland'" in *Southern Punch* (13 February 1864) took up the issue, but in the Confederacy it had nothing to do with Union politics or even abolition, but, as always, everything to do with coldhearted Yankee penny-pinching.

◊ ◊ ◊

In the North, the question soon became not just what to do with the contraband but what *he* might do. That is, his having crossed the line to freedom heightened the white fears that other lines would be crossed, not only social and political ones but sexual ones as well. Before the war, the black urban dandy Zip Coon had appeared in minstrelsy at about the same time as and in contrast to the raggedy slave Jim Crow.[3] Dressed to the exaggerated nines, Zip Coon exudes what he believes to be sartorial virility and gentility and boasts of feminine conquests that fool no one but himself. In antebellum America, his social and romantic pretensions were kept in place ("qualified," as Lott [1993] says) by the literary conventions of that caricature, conventions

DRAFTS.

Gentleman of Color.—"YAH! YAH! DARKEY HAB DE BEST OB IT NOW. DAR'S DE WHITE MAN'S DRAFF, AND HERE'S DE NIGGAH'S!"

"Drafts." Courtesy of the Library of Congress.

that made him explicitly a "coon," implicitly a slave. A war against a slave-holding nation and the contraband blacks who had thrown off the chains of slavery to go North, however, created a new reality not so easily constrained. That speaker in "The Contraband's Lament" is no Zip Coon strutting his ridiculous stuff on stage. As he says, the ladies in St. Louis "say I'm cupid, don't you see?" but the author defuses the implicit threat with the contraband's departure.

The question of what contrabands might do also brought to the surface apprehensions about African Americans already in the North. The cartoon "Drafts," *Vanity Fair* (26 July 1862), illustrates the threat graphically and unequivocally. In the foreground and etched in careful detail, the "Gentleman of Color" cools his heels in the shade, while white soldiers sketched lightly in the background march off to war. In contrast to the antebellum minstrel stereotype of the black dandy, his pretensions laughable, this black man represents the new order: well dressed, muscular, and attractive. And unlike the speaker in "The Contraband's Lament," this "darkey," as he puts it, has no intention of going back where he belongs—he appears to "belong" in the North— and has no reason to leave. Loafing and inviting his soul, drink in hand, he has much to look forward to: "Dar's de white man's draff, and here's de niggah's!"

Published three months after the Emancipation Proclamation, the panel of six cartoons titled "Quashee's Dream of Emancipation," in *Frank Leslie's Illustrated Newspaper* (March 1863), presents a puzzling, because conflicted, collation of the political, social, and economic implications of freed blacks. The first panel is the familiar turnabout of master over slave and not so much a dream as a reality given the promise of freedom for contraband slaves soon after the war began. Quashee's dreams that follow examine what he might do with that freedom, white "nightmares" that visual comedy wants to make laughable.

In the second and fifth cartoons, the highly starched collars and formal clothing, like the military uniform of the "brigade general" in the fourth panel, exaggerate the grotesquely Negroid look of the black men who, therefore, are not to be taken seriously; they are "contained." The third dream is very different, suggesting the ultimate white (male) nightmare of free black men: not only do they want white women, but white women want them. The African American here is no laughable minstrel caricature, but a black man smoldering with unmistakable sexuality fueled by alcohol, his right to this good life encouraged by

QUASHEE'S DREAM OF EMANCIPATION.

He dreams that massa and he exchange positions, as above.

He dreams that he is feted at Washington, and solicited to stand for Congress.

He dreams that the young missis humbly waits upon him while he reads the Tribune.

He imagines himself a Brigadier-General seated in a stagebox at Wallack's Theatre.

He dreams that all the light and easy employments at the North and elsewhere fall into his mouth.

He awakes to find that Emancipation hasn't much altered his position after all.

"Quashee's Dream of Emancipation." Courtesy of the American Antiquarian Society.

reading the *New York Tribune*, Horace Greeley's journalistic forum for Radical Republicanism. (He is not looking at help wanted ads.) All the more shocking to nineteenth-century readers would be the pretty, genteel white woman (not the stereotypically homely female abolitionist) who "humbly," the caption reports (and without apparent resistance), prepares his meal. In the last cartoon, then, were readers to sympathize with Quashee's lot? Or does he deserve the horse-whipping, not because he is a slave but because of his dreams? Did white readers, then, have the last laugh? On Quashee?

◊ ◊ ◊

Enlisting blacks as soldiers was the most significant change that the war created in the place of African Americans, which in turn forced a re-examination of that place. Many abolitionists had urged recruiting African Americans from the beginning, blacks had tried to enlist, and individual commanders in the field, such as John Fremont and David Hunter, had authorized training black troops early on.[4] As Commander in Chief, always cautious not to alienate border states, Lincoln countermanded every effort, his caution reflected as well in the Emancipation Proclamation that freed slaves only in Confederate states. More radical and more immediate in its effect was a brief addition to the proclamation as officially issued in January 1863: "And I further declare and make known, that such persons of suitable condition will be received into the armed service of the United States to garrison forts, positions, stations, and other places, and to man vessels of all sorts in said service." Some in the Confederacy, most notably General Robert E. Lee, had long argued for enlisting slaves as soldiers, and the Confederate Congress debated it heatedly late in the war. A cartoon in *Frank Leslie's Illustrated Newspaper* (1 April 1865) had some fun with the dilemma faced by the beleaguered enemy.

Confederate editors railed and raged at the Union for making soldiers of African Americans, most of them contraband (over half by war's end), but the cartoon "Birds of a Feather" in *Southern Punch* (5 December 1863) found it another occasion for satirically portraying the usual lame-brained Yankee. Despite his name, this Sambo is no slave caricature, but a nattily dressed, prosperously proportioned fellow not about to fall for the blandishments of the Yankee recruiter.

Blacks who did so received the blistering derision of a writer in the *Richmond Examiner* in 1863 reporting their actions in a fictitious battle.

GREAT FIGHT OVER THE NIGGER IN THE REBEL CONGRESS—
TRAGIC RESULT.

"Great Fight over the Nigger in the Rebel Congress—Tragic Result." Courtesy of Special Collections/Musselman Library, Gettysburg College.

"Birds of a Feather."

YANKEE GENERAL.—Now Sambo, I have made you Captain of the Odoriferous Guards. You are to attack the Rebels wherever you meet them.

SAMBO.—Yes, massa. But de Ribils fight mighty hard, and if dey ketch me, I's a gone darkey.

YANKEE GENERAL.—You must struggle for victory; fight till you die.

SAMBO.—Yes massa! I always do dat! *Aside.* I's gwine to git out ob dis. Ole missus used to say dat white men dat puts demselves on 'quality with niggar, no better dan niggar demselves. De fust chance I gits, I's gwine to gib de slip to all de black guards of Brudder Abe. Aint ready to gib up de ghost yit.

"Birds of a Feather." Courtesy of The Library of Virginia.

The *Harrisburg (Pennsylvania) Patriot and Union* (26 February 1863) reprinted it as "The First Great Negro Battle," a "laughable description of the first great battle to be fought, it is supposed, by the colored army to supply the places of the 300,000 white soldiers whose term of service will expire in May."

> The fate of the negro, of the white population at the South, and of the Northern army, respectively, will be decided in a brief contest, which will occur about the middle of next June, and which we will describe as gravely and succinctly as possible. On the 1st of April, fifty thousand negroes, who have been previously drilled in various camps of instruction, will be debarked at Aquia creek. . . . But it will require at least six weeks of toil to perform this simple feat. It is at last accomplished. . . . The skirmishers of the Grand Colored Division are thrown out. They deploy.
>
> The voice of an overseer calling hogs is heard in a distant field. They rally in the reserve. No rebels being visible, they are again thrown forward. They feel for the enemy, but he is not to be felt. They fire at nothing, fifty feet in the air, and hit it every time. The rebels being thus driven to their earthworks, the Grand Colored Division advances at the *pas de charge*, singing a Methodist refrain, to storm the enemy's position, and to "carry the crest" at all hazards. Of a sudden, the artillery of A. P. Hill's command belches forth a hurricane of shell and shrapnel. There is a rising of wool, as of quills upon the fretful porcupine, under the caps of dusky brigadiers and sooty major generals; there is a simultaneous effusion of mellifluous perspiration from fifty thousand tarry hides; there is a display of ivory like fifty thousand flashes of lightning; fifty thousand pairs of charcoal knees are knocking together, and one hundred thousand Ethiopian eyeballs are rolling madly in their sockets, like so many drunken and distracted moons dancing in an ebon sky.

Peace Democrats in the North argued that enlisting black soldiers, along with the Emancipation Proclamation in general, was yet another piece of the grand Republican scheme for racial equality. The majority in the North had no altruistic agenda of true citizenship for African Americans, even as soldiers, but two years of war had strained manpower, casualties were high, and if victory meant the end of slavery, should not the black man play a part in that, even die for that cause?

The best-known comic answer to such questions was Charles Hal-pine's "Sambo's Right to be Kilt." As adjutant to General David Hunter ("Lincoln's Abolitionist General," his biographer calls him),[5] Halpine had drawn up his commanding officer's order in May 1862 to organize a black regiment in South Carolina, then wrote a poem to quell the opposition the order provoked among the largely Irish, New York regulars. Irish himself and a former writer for the *New York Irish American*, Halpine knew well a constituency more racist than most Northerners. "Miles O'Reilly" was one of "them," and, as William Hanchett says, "his reasoning could persuade whites to accept blacks as soldiers without in the least disturbing their fundamental prejudices to blacks" (1970, 70). Miles told it like it was:

> Some tell us 'tis a burnin' shame
> To make the naygers fight;
> And that the thrade of bein' kilt
> Belongs but to the white:
> But as for me, upon my sowl!
> So liberal are we here,
> I'll let Sambo be murthered instead of myself,
> On every day in the year.

The second stanza continues in that vein, and if only these stanzas are referenced, as they usually are, Halpine's point of view appears intolerant and intolerable. But Miles is the speaker here, a mask that Halpine drops in the third stanza to challenge hypocritical, sanctimonious objections to blacks as soldiers.

> The men who object to Sambo
> Should take his place and fight;
> And it's betther to have a nayger's hue
> Than a liver that's wake an' white.
> Though Sambo's black as the ace of spades,
> His finger a thrigger can pull,
> And his eye runs sthraight on the barrel-sights
> From undher its thatch of wool.

With "A Consistent Negrophobist," *Harper's Weekly* (16 August 1862) embraced black enlistment without irony, a response to the Militia Act

A CONSISTENT NEGROPHOBIST.

DROWNING GENTLEMAN. "Take that Rope away, you darned Nigger! What decent White Man, do you suppose, is going to allow himself to be saved by a confounded Nig——" (*Goes down, consistent to the last.*)

"A Consistent Negrophibist." Courtesy of Special Collections, University of Virginia Library.

that Congress had passed in July 1862, authorizing the president to employ "persons of African descent" in military service. (Lincoln chose not to do so.) *Harper's* usually took a compassionate view of black Americans, and here the foolishly consistent, "decent White Man" gets caricatured, not the black man who offers to save him.

Blackface caricature prevailed in the popular media, though, even when used to champion black soldiers. "Number One," from a series titled "Kulllud Sermons, Addressed to the Black Brigade, by our Sooty

Chaplain," in *Phunny Phellow* (January 1865), does not simply echo white patriotism but salutes the bravery of the soldiers of the "Black Brigade" themselves.[6]

> Dat ar flag witch flotes so splendiferusly above dis camp you hab borne brabely fru de tickest ob de fite. Dis indiwidoowal watch you from de safe side ob a big tree. You bore de brunt ob de battle— wite sojers wa'nt nowhar! You smoted de Filistine—dat is de rebs—wid yer pistils, sabers and baggynets. Darfo, in de lang-widge ob Youllesis de Grate, you conkered de enemy and put dem hoss dem combar!

We can laugh at the way the timid chaplain speaks but not at what he says about the courage of African American soldiers. For the white author, that comic way of speaking masks not only his praise of black troops but also his quick but pointed criticism of white soldiers.

By 1865, black soldiers had, in fact, acquitted themselves well, and newspaper reports of their mettle in the battles of Port Hudson and Milliken's Bend in mid-1863 had much to do with answering the early, oft-repeated slander that "the nigger won't fight." An "Ethiopian Song and Chorus Performed by Wood's Minstrels," the 1863 sheet music "Who Says the Darkies Wont Fight?" could answer factually and affirmatively.

> Some white folks have been heard to say
> De niggers would not fight,
> But I guess dat dey look at it now quite in another light,
> Hush up your mouf you "Copperheads" don't take dat for a
>   plea;
> To keep us from de battle field where all ob you should be.

The black speaker makes the retort to cowardly Copperheads all the more pungent. Other verses point to early battles in which black soldiers had proven themselves and to their eager anticipation of taking on the former "massa."

Success also made it possible to bring to the fore long-standing racist "truths." The speaker in Mary Ann Kidder's sheet music "Dey Said We Wouldn't Fight" (circa 1864, music by Effie Susan Parkhurst) took on the libel that blacks were incapable of both the discipline and rigors of soldiering.

"Babylon Is Fallen." Courtesy of the Lester S. Levy Collection, The Sheridan Libraries, The Johns Hopkins University.

Dey said we wouldn't fight,
Kase we's born so awful black,
Kase we's lazy from de cranum to de toes,
But dey'll find dese darkies some
When de rebel sojers come,
If dey'll keep us well in powder for de foes.

Speakers in both songs talk the talk of the minstrel stereotype, but they are anti-types—not lazy, not cowards, not slaves, but men, men ready to fight. As always, the personas were the creations of white writers, but they voiced how many African Americans must have felt, making the case for a people who did not have a voice of their own in popular culture.

The reality of black soldiers also gave new meaning to the laughable reversal of master and slave. The words to Henry Clay Work's sheet music "Babylon Is Fallen" (1863) evoke weak grins at best, but the cover illustration has some visual fun with former slaves, now armed and fitted out as Union troops, taking gleeful potshots at the retreating slave master. The abolitionist George Root would have found the turnabout not simply comic but a triumph of what was right, yet for the majority of his countrymen, the reversal itself was humorous enough, as in "Fun for the Family" in *Frank Leslie's Illustrated Newspaper* (25 February 1865):

> The siege of Nashville [December 1864] was the occasion of some laughable incidents, as the following paragraph from a correspondence written in that city shows: "During the skirmish in the little reconnaissance made by Gen. Steedman on our left, a couple of soldiers of the colored brigade came upon three rebels, whose guns were unloaded, and demanded their surrender. One of the Johnnies indignantly refused to surrender to a 'd—d nigger.' 'Berry sorry, massa,' said Sambo, bringing his piece to a 'ready;' 'but we's in a great hurry, and hain't got no time to send for a white man!' The ominous click that accompanied this remark brought the scion of chivalry to time, and he was brought in, crying and swearing all the way that his father would kill him if he ever heard that he had surrendered to a nigger."

Freedom, though, or any kind of new, meaningful place in white society, for that matter, is not at issue here: the incident is "laughable" as the writer says, "Fun for the Family" as the editor says, because it reduces this former "scion of chivalry" to a blubbering coward, and all the more humorous because the rifle-wielding former slave does so in the dialect of the minstrel slave caricature Sambo.

African Americans comprised nearly 10 percent of the Union forces at war's end, 57 percent of them from slave states (Smith 2002, 8), but the Confederate surrender in May 1865 meant no victory for them. Slavery ended, but efforts to give African Americans the rights of citizens with the Thirteenth (1865), Fourteenth (1868), and Fifteenth (1870) Amendments to the Constitution met with resistance in the North as well as the South. (Those rights would not be fully realized for another century, with the Civil Rights Act of 1964.) Sentimental engravings published at war's end honored black veterans, a crutch replacing an amputated leg, moving icons of their sacrifice. But a cartoon published in *Yankee Notions* (June 1865) a month after the end of the war reflects more accurately the popular imagination regarding African Americans, even those who had shouldered arms for the Union. The message

"Sambo on a New Footing." From *Yankee Notions* (June 1865).

in the balloon is unclear, but not that of the black soldier thumbing his nose at the Confederate president, which recalls the runaway slave in the 1861 lithograph "The (Fort) Monroe Doctrine." Uniformed, armed, and fully equipped, this black man has played a part in the Union victory; and with the war over, the "new footing" would seem to auger well for the next step, some kind of meaningful acknowledgement of his contribution to that victory. And yet, decked out though he is, with all the accoutrements of a real soldier, his regulation uniform ends with tattered pant legs that lead the eye to his prominently splayed bare feet and elongated heels. With the end of the war, he may not be a slave, but with his flat nose, big lips, wooly hair, and those feet, he is a minstrel caricature, still the same old Sambo and still on the same old footing.

In the decades following the war, the conventions of blackface caricature would persist in portraying the African American in popular culture. Blacks did replace white performers in minstrelsy after the war, but they performed the comical and sentimental renditions of the good old antebellum days that white audiences wanted to see and hear. Lampoons of black soldiers also became popular set pieces on the minstrel stage as a closing hurrah of the performance that showcased precision music and drill performances. The 1881 sheet music for the "Coonville Guards Parade," composed for Haverly's Minstrels, portrayed black performers in a self-mocking account of more parading than soldiering, more partying than patriotism: "When balls fly around, we're not to be found, / We much prefer running away." As Robert Toll writes, "Whatever they [the guards] might seem, the songs seem to say, these were not military men; they were party-loving blacks" (1974, 250), creating a world in which the war had never happened. A black performer in an interview in the *New York Clipper* (4 March 1882) put it in his best minstrel way of speaking: "De darkey will be hisself once more and forget dat he eber had any trouble." The blackface was now real, but it was still a mask.

Notes

Introduction

1. In truth, though, the Union blockade of the Confederacy had long put materials of all kinds in short supply. "Toward the end of the war," Willard A. and Porter W. Heaps write, "paper of Confederate imprints was so thin that printing on the reverse side made reading difficult, and copies could no longer be stood upright on the piano music rack without support." Willard A. Heaps and Porter W. Heaps, *The Singing Sixties: The Spirit of Civil War Days Drawn from the Music of the Times* (Norman: Univ. of Oklahoma Press, 1960), 9.

2. The single best source of information on humor periodicals is David E. E. Sloane, ed., *American Humor Magazines and Comic Periodicals* (New York: Greenwood, 1987).

Chapter One

1. Highly scurrilous material of all kinds circulated in handwritten form. A version of the 1863 published broadside "Jeff Davis' Dream" is a sexual and scatological account of the president and his wife in bed. See Thomas P. Lowry, *The Story the Soldiers Wouldn't Tell; Sex in the Civil War* (Mechanicsburg, PA: Stackpole, 1994), 49–50.

2. A good account of the affair is "The Belle of Richmond" in Mark E. Neely Jr., Harold Holzer, and Gabor S. Boritt, *The Confederate Image, Prints of the Lost Cause* (Chapel Hill: Univ. of North Carolina Press, 1987), 79–96.

3. Paul M. Zall, ed., *Abe Lincoln's Legacy of Laughter* (Knoxville: Univ. of Tennessee Press, 2007), cites the Salem, Illinois, *Advertiser* (19 November 1863) as an earlier source, but I have not been able to verify that.

4. In Kenneth A. Bernard, *Lincoln and the Music of the Civil War* (Caldwell, IN: Caxton, 1966), 260.

5. Ibid., 243–276; Bernard documents in detail what he calls the "Antietam Incident."

6. Quoted in Bernard, *Lincoln and the Music of the Civil War*, 259.

7. For the many and diverse opinions of Lincoln in the decades following the war, see the last two chapters of Michael Davis's *The Image of Lincoln in the South*. For some in the South, enmity has continued into the twenty-first century. In Richmond, Virginia, in April 2003, at the unveiling of the first statue of Lincoln

below the Mason Dixon Line, protestors booed and hissed while a plane flew over the ceremony displaying a banner reading "Sic Temper Tyrannis!" the words attributed to John Wilkes Booth upon shooting the president.

Chapter Two

1. *Songs of Humor and Sentiment* (Richmond: J. W. Randolph, 1863), 6–7.

2. Taylor M. Camberlin, Bronwen C. Souders, and John M. Souders, eds., *The Waterford News* (Waterford, VA: Waterford Foundation, 1999). All quotations of the *Waterford News* are from this facsimile publication.

Chapter Three

1. J. P. Robens, preface, *The Old Flag, First Published by Union Prisoners at Camp Ford, Tyler, Texas* (New York: n.p., 1864).

2. William Howard Merrell, *Five Months in Rebeldom* (Rochester, NY: Adams and Dabney, 1862), 26–29. Merrell, in Libby Prison after the first battle at Bull Run, attributes the poem to "Sergeant Solomon Wood, of the 27th Regiment." It was also published as a broadside, probably in Richmond, as "Prison Bill of Fare. By a Prisoner of War. Composed, Written and Spoken at the Exhibition of the Prisoners of War Dramatic Association, Richmond, Va., Nov. 8th, 1861."

3. George Root followed up his success with two sequels in 1863, "On the Field of Battle, Mother" and "Just After the Battle, Mother." A World War I parody was titled "Just Behind the Battle, Mother."

4. See W. W. Carnes, "Here's Your Mule," in Bromfield L. Ridley, *Battles and Sketches of the Army of Tennessee* (Mexico, MO: Missouri Printing and Publishing, 1906), 633–634; and William Shepard Walsh, *Handy-book of Literary Curiosities* (Philadelphia: Lippincott, 1892), 753.

5. Richard Harwell, *Songs of the Confederacy* (New York: Broadcast Music, 1951), 92, says, "The phrase probably had its origin in the disappearance of stock at the approach" of the famous Confederate raider John Morgan and his men, but we know the phrase was "popular" in October 1861, several months before Morgan and his raids became famous. Frank W. Hoogerwerf, *Confederate Sheet-Music Imprints* (Brooklyn: Institute for Studies in American Music, 1984), 53, notes that a stanza referring to Morgan was pasted in copies sold to Confederates who bought C. D. Benson's 1862 "Here's Your Mule." In 1864 C. D. Benson capitalized on Morgan's fame with the sheet "How Are You? John Morgan," "a sequel to 'Here's Your Mule'" that featured on the title page a picture of the Confederate general on a mule in his heralded escape from an Ohio prison in 1863.

6. Wiley, *Life of Johnny Reb*, 382, n. 48, quotes the manuscript diary of Augustas L. P. Viarin regarding the origin of the joke. "The first I heard of it ['Here's your mule'] was this—some man in the neighborhood had lost an old gray mule and was . . . enquiring for it among the Regiments—Co. B. had straw

in their tents to sleep on. . . . Among them Tom Nance . . . his hair was very thin on his head and his ears seemed all the larger for it—Under the general excitement of the day he laid down in his tent to sleep—some lively fellows roving about . . . happened to look in Tom's tent and being struck with his appearance called out for the mule man—Here's your mule others came to see and repeated the saying . . . alover [sic] the camp and those adjoining and became a by word everywhere." Wiley says the entry is undated, "but evidently late 1861."

7. The parody was composed by a soldier in an Iowa regiment in 1861, according to John Billings, *Hardtack and Coffee: The Unwritten Story of Army Life* (Boston: Smith, 1887), 118–119.

8. E. Lawrence Abel, *Singing the New Nation* (Mechanicsburg, PA: Stackpole, 2000), 330, n. 42, says that "the last lines ('I wish the war was over . . .' indicate it was sung before then [1866]."

9. The lyrics were written by John Alcée Augustin, a soldier in the Confederate Army of Tennessee, and included in his book of poems published shortly after the close of the war. The poem is dated "In the Field Near Dalton, Ga. Dec. 22, 1863."

Chapter Four

1. Robert C. Toll, *Blacking Up: The Minstrel Show in Nineteenth-Century America* (New York: Oxford Univ. Press, 1974), 247; Caroline Moseley, "'When Will Dis Cruel War Be Ober?': Attitudes Toward Blacks in Popular Song of the Civil War, "*American Music* 2 (Fall 1984): 6; and Kate Masur, "'A Rare Phenomenon of Philological Vegetation': The Word 'Contraband' and the Meanings of Emancipation in the United States," *Journal of American History* 93 (2007): 1074, n. 43. The popular tenor Frank Crumit recorded the song for Victor in 1927, and the tune appeared in Jerome Kern's 1921 musical *Good Morning, Dearie*.

2. For a thorough analysis of the contraband in its many manifestations, see Masur, "'A Rare Phenomenon of Philological Vegetation,'" 1050–1084. Fahs, *Imagined Civil War,* 151–162, discusses the contraband in several literary genres.

3. For the background of Zip Coon and other blackface dandy characterizations and their place in antebellum American culture, see William J. Mahar, *Behind the Burnt Cork Mask* (Urbana: Univ. of Illinois Press, 1999), 203–209; Cockrell, *Demons of Disorder,* 1977, 92–139; and Barbara Lewis, "Daddy Blue: The Evolution of the Dark Dandy," in *Inside the Minstrel Mask: Readings in Nineteenth-Century Blackface Minstrelsy*, ed. Annemarie Bean et al. (Middletown, CO: Wesleyan Univ. Press, 1996), 256–272.

4. Dudley Taylor Cornish, *The Sable Arm: Negro Troops in the Union Army, 1861–1865* (New York: Norton, 1966), recounts the many and varied efforts to this end.

5. Edward A. Miller Jr., *Lincoln's Abolitionist General, the Biography of David Hunter* (Columbia: Univ. of South Carolina Press, 1997).

6. The official name given to the first formal military, but non-combatant, unit of African Americans in Cincinnati in 1862, "Black Brigade," became the term used for black troops generally.

References

Abel, E. Lawrence. 2000. *Singing the New Nation*. Mechanicsburg, PA: Stackpole.

Berry, Stephen W. 1998. "When Mail Was Armor, Envelopes of the Great Rebellion." *Southern Cultures* 4 (3): 63–83.

Bickham, William. 1863. *Rosencrans' Campaign with the 14th Army Corps*. Cincinnati: Moore, Wilstash, Keys.

Chamberlin, Taylor M., Bronwen C. Souders, and John M. Souders, eds. 1999. *The Waterford News*. Waterford, VA: Waterford Foundation.

Chesnut, Mary. 1981. *Mary Chesnut's Civil War*. Edited by C. Vann Woodward. New Haven: Yale Univ. Press.

Cockrell, Dale. 1977. *Demons of Disorder: Early Blackface Minstrels and Their World*. New York: Cambridge Univ. Press.

Davis, Michael. 1971. *The Image of Lincoln in the South*. Knoxville: Univ. of Tennessee Press.

Fahs, Alice. 2001. *The Imagined Civil War: Popular Literature of the North & South, 1861–1865*. Chapel Hill: Univ. of North Carolina Press.

Faust, Drew Gilpin. 1988. *The Creation of Confederate Nationalism, Ideology, and Identity in the Civil War South*. Baton Rouge: Louisiana State Univ. Press.

Freemantle, Sir Arthur James Lyon. 1863. *Three Months in the Southern States*. London: Blackwood.

Godfrey, John A. 1862. *Rhymed Tactics*. New York: Nostrand.

Hanchett, William. 1970. *Irish: Charles G. Halpine in Civil War America*. Syracuse, NY: Syracuse Univ. Press.

Hardee, Lt. Col. J. W. 1861. *Rifle and Light Infantry Tactics*. Vol. 1. Philadelphia: Lippincott.

Harris, Brayton. 1999. *Blue and Gray in Black and White: Newspapers in the Civil War*. Dulles, VA: Batsford Brassey.

Harwell, Richard B. 1950. *Confederate Music*. Chapel Hill: Univ. of North Carolina Press.

Hesseltine, William Best. 1930. *Civil War Prisons, a Study in War Psychology*. New York: Frederick Unger.

Holmes, Oliver Wendell. 1891. *Pages from an Old Volume of Life*. Boston: Houghton, Mifflin.

Jackson, Walter M. 1954. *The Story of Selma*. Birmingham, AL: Birmingham Printing.

Lee, Ruth Webb. 1952. *A History of Valentines, 1860–1865*. New York: Crowell.

Lott, Eric. 1993. *Love and Theft: Blackface Minstrelsy and the American Working Class*. New York: Oxford Univ. Press.

Massey, Mary Elizabeth. 1966. *Bonnet Brigades*. New York: Knopf.

———. 1993. *Ersatz in the Confederacy; Shortages and Substitutes on the Southern Homefront*. Columbia: Univ. of South Carolina Press. (Orig. pub. 1952.)

Moore, Frank, ed. 1862. *The Rebellion Record: A Diary of American Events*. Vol. 5. New York: Putnam.

Nickels, Cameron. 1993. *New England Humor from the Revolutionary War to the Civil War*. Knoxville: Univ. of Tennessee Press.

Only Authentic Life of Abraham Lincoln, Alias "Old Abe." [1864]. New York: Haney.

Osterweis, Rollin G. 1949. *Romanticism and Nationalism in the Old South*. New Haven: Yale Univ. Press.

Peterson, Merrill. 1994. *Lincoln in American Memory*. New York: Oxford Univ. Press.

Root, George. 1891. *The Story of a Musical Life: An Autobiography*. Cincinnati: John Church.

Schmidt, Leigh Eric. 1995. *Consumer Rites: The Buying and Selling of American Holidays*. Princeton: Princeton Univ. Press.

Silber, Nina. 1993. *The Romance of Reunion: Northerners and the South: 1865–1900*. Chapel Hill: Univ. of North Carolina Press.

Smith, John David, ed. 2002. *Black Soldiers in Blue: African-American Troops in the Civil War*. Chapel Hill: Univ. of North Carolina Press.

Staff, Frank. 1966. *The Picture Postcard and Its Origin*. New York: Praeger.

Taylor, William R. 1961. *Cavalier and Yankee: The Old South and American National Character*. New York: Braziller.

Toll, Robert C. 1974. *Blacking Up: The Minstrel Show in Nineteenth-Century America*. New York: Oxford Univ. Press.

Voss, Frederick S. 1988. "Aldabert Volck: The Confederate Answer to Thomas Nast." *Smithsonian Studies in American Art* 2 (3): 67–87.

Ward, Artemus [Charles Farrar Browne]. 1865. *Artemus Ward; His Travels*. New York: Carelton.

Weiss, William R., Jr. 1995. *The Catalog of Union Civil War Patriotic Covers*. Bethlehem, PA: Weiss.

Wiley, Bell I. 1943. *The Life of Johnny Reb: The Common Soldier of the Confederacy*. Indianapolis: Bobbs-Merrill.

———. 1952. *The Life of Billy Yank, the Common Soldier of the Union*. Indianapolis: Bobbs-Merrill.

Wishnietsky, Benjamin. 1991. *Confederate Patriotic Covers and Their Uses*. North Miami: David G. Philips.

Wood, Forrest G. 1970. *Black Scare: The Racist Response to Emancipation and Reconstruction*. Berkeley: Univ. of California Press.

Zall, Paul M., ed. 1982. *Abe Lincoln Laughing*. Berkeley: Univ. of California Press.

Index